Fundraising
for your school

Other Easy Step-by-Step Guides in the series include:

Telemarketing, Cold Calling and Appointment Making

Marketing

Stress and Time Management

Motivating Your Staff

Recruiting the Right Staff

Better Budgeting for your Business

Building a Positive Media Profile

Writing Advertising Copy

Writing Articles and Newsletters

Managing Change

Handling Confrontation

Giving Confident Presentations

Being Positive and Staying Positive

Successful Selling

Communicating with More Confidence

Fewer, Shorter, Better Meetings

All the above guides are available from:

Rowmark Limited
65 Rogers Mead
Hayling Island
Hampshire
England PO11 0PL
Telephone: 023 9246 1931
Fax: 023 9246 0574
enquiries@rowmark.co.uk
www.rowmark.co.uk

Easy Step by Step Guide

Fundraising for your school

Pauline Rowson

Rowmark

Published by Rowmark Limited
65 Rogers Mead
Hayling Island
Hampshire
England
PO11 0PL

ISBN 0 9548045 2 X

Copyright © Pauline Rowson 2005

The right of Pauline Rowson to be identified as the author of this work has been asserted by her in accordance with the Copyright, Design and Patents Act 1988.

Note: The material contained in this book is set out in good faith for general guidance and no liability can be accepted for loss or expense incurred as a result of relying in particular circumstances on statements made in this book.

All rights reserved. No part of this publication may be reproduced in any material form (including photocopying or storing it in any medium by electronic means and whether or not transiently or incidentally to some other use of publication) without the written permission of the copyright owner except in accordance with the provisions of the Copyright, Designs and Patents Act 1988 or under the terms of a licence issued by the Copyright Licensing Agency Ltd. 90 Tottenham Court Road, London, England W1P 9HE. Applications for the copyright owner's written permission to reproduce any part of this publication should be addressed to the publisher.

Warning: The doing of an unauthorised act in relation to a copyright work may result in both a civil claim for damages and criminal prosecution.

Typeset by Freelance Publishing Services, Brinscall, Lancs

Printed in Great Britain by RPM Reprographics Ltd. Chichester

Contents

About the author	x
Introduction	1
How to use this guide	2
What you will learn from this guide	2
1 The climate for fundraising	3
Why do we need to fundraise?	4
Different areas of funding	5
Some questions to ask	7
In summary	7
2 What are you fundraising for?	9
How to persuade the sceptics	10
Your wish list	12
An example wish list	13
Put a cost against each item	14
Allocate a time scale	15
Potential funders and time scales	16
In summary	18
3 Organizing for fundraising	19
Engage an external fundraiser	19

	Employ a fundraiser	21
	Do it yourself	22
	Appoint someone within the school	23
	In summary	24
4	**Registering as a charity**	25
	Do we need to register as a charity?	25
	Do I need a separate bank account?	27
	Appointing Trustees/Committee members	28
	In summary	31
5	**Preparation and writing your appeal**	33
	Researching	34
	Give your appeal a name	37
	Writing the appeal	38
	In summary	42
6	**Sources of funding – trusts, foundations and grants**	45
	Researching potential funders	45
	Raising money from trusts and foundations	51
	Writing the appeal letter	53
	In summary	56
7	**Sources of funding – magazines and newspapers**	59
	Carry out a survey of who reads what	59
	Train your readers to look for relevant articles	60
	Identifying a connection	61

	How to approach them	63
	In summary	64
8	**Sources of funding – the rich and famous**	**65**
	Who are they?	65
	How do you find them?	66
	How do you approach them?	69
	In summary	70
9	**Sources of funding – businesses**	**73**
	Who are they?	73
	How do you find them?	74
	Build a database	77
	How do you approach them?	77
	What businesses are looking for	78
	What can you offer them?	79
	List the benefits	81
	Define the deal	82
	Do you offer sole sponsorship?	83
	The letter to businesses	83
	An example letter	88
	In summary	90
10	**Approaching sponsors by telephone**	**91**
	Getting past the telephonist	92
	Set your objective	94
	The stages of the call	95

Opening the call		95
Asking questions and presenting benefits		97
Buying signals		99
Closing the call		99
In summary		100

11 The face to face meeting — 103

Who should go?	104
Set your objectives	104
Have the right material	105
Buying motivations	106
Opening the conversation	107
Selling benefits	109
Getting a commitment	110
In summary	110

12 Giving a presentation — 113

Overcoming nerves	114
Preparing your presentation	115
Watch your body language	116
Some openings	117
The ending	117
A word about questions	118
In summary	119

13 Building a media profile — 121

What is newsworthy?	122
Who will be interested?	123

How to get on television and radio	124
Writing the news release	124
Laying out the news release	129
Photographs	130
Some rules for good media relations	131
In summary	132

14 Other ways of raising funds — 135

Don't fall foul of the law	135
Street collections	135
Carol singing	137
House to house collections	137
Collection boxes	138
Lotteries	138
Free prize draws	139
Prize competitions	140
In summary	141

15 Keep going — 143

Always look for opportunities	143
Network	143
Read the national press	144
Maintain your media profile	144
Build your database	144
Say thank you promptly	145

Useful addresses — 147

About the author

Pauline Rowson has worked with many schools in the south of England and has trained a vast number of education professionals at all levels.

She has advised schools on management and fundraising issues and was instrumental in helping one state school in Portsmouth raise £1.5 million.

Her background is in marketing and the media and she has worked for charities both regional and national. She is author of several books on marketing, selling and personal development.

Introduction

When the staff of Priory Secondary School in Portsmouth decided to raise £1.5 million it didn't cross their minds that they couldn't do it and thus the CAN DO Appeal was born. Eighteen months later the school succeeded in raising £1 million. It has since gone on to raise a further £1.5 million and is now a Specialist Sports College.

Priory has succeeded where many schools fail – why? How did they go about it? And where did the money come from?

One of the critical factors that contributed to Priory's success was their willingness to take advice. Priory was also prepared to speculate to accumulate. It was a gamble that paid off for the 1,200 pupil school, based in inner city Portsmouth. Now many schools are looking for additional finance not only to help them stretch already tight budgets but also to enhance their links with those outside education.

How to use this guide

This guide is written in as clear a style as possible to help you. I recommend that you read it through from beginning to end and then dip into it to refresh your memory. The boxes in each chapter contain tips to help you. Also at the end of each chapter is a handy summary of the points covered.

What you will learn from this guide:

- how to identify opportunities for funding within your school
- how to organize your resources for effective fundraising
- how to identify and research the various sources of funding
- how to approach different funders
- how to write an appeal document
- how to cold call potential funders
- how to sell to potential funders

Note: to avoid confusion and the cumbersome use of 'he' or 'she' throughout the guide, 'he' has been adopted throughout. No prejudice is intended.

1
The climate for fundraising

Private schools have been in the business of fundraising for very much longer than state schools but times have changed and are changing. When I first started running fundraising courses for schools some years ago I met quite a lot of resistance from head teachers and others who didn't think it was 'right' that they should have to get out the 'begging bowl' in order to generate enough cash to run their schools. Indeed I didn't think it was right but I recognized, just as they very quickly did, that in today's climate, in order to succeed and provide the best for pupils, a school needs not only to generate extra cash but also vital cash. It also needs to work in co-operation with its local community and the business community.

Today the whole arena of fundraising has changed not only for schools but also for national charities. The corporate sector is now looking for something 'in return for their money'. Schools can provide that. Indeed they have a great deal to offer the business community and the wider community. Schools are in a strong position to forge mutually beneficial links with organizations. Never before have there been so many opportunities for schools to raise money and gain additional support for initiatives (the good news) but never before has the competition been so fierce (the bad news).

Therefore in order to succeed schools need to adopt a very professional approach to fundraising. It is not enough to identify a need and then scrabble around trying to find the money; this is not only time-consuming but is also exhausting for everyone concerned. It certainly is not the best use of a valued member of staff's time.

> By adopting a professional approach from the outset, by doing your research and preparing thoroughly you can save yourself a great deal of time and energy and guarantee a higher rate of success.

Why do we need to fundraise?

Here are some reasons; you may come up with others.

- to help stretch our existing budgets
- to buy new equipment
- to upgrade the school buildings
- to refurbish the school
- to attain specialist school status
- to provide additional specialist staff
- to take children on outings

- to enable us to conduct more activities within the school
- to provide more facilities for the local community

Whatever your reasons for fundraising you must be prepared for hard work; also be prepared for it to take time. My experience of working with many schools has taught me that many are too unrealistic about the time it takes to raise money. It can take months of painstaking effort, years even, so you should therefore view fundraising for your school as an ongoing activity, indeed a fact of school life.

> Fundraising is like a snowball; it gathers momentum as you go along. Once you have a track record of successful fundraising you will find others will give and it gets easier.

Different areas of funding

There are four broad areas to fundraising for schools.

Educational

this covers things like providing materials for school, for example exercise books.

Sponsorship

raising sponsors for school events, trips, class competitions, prize giving etc, where in return for a company giving money the school will promote that organisation through advertising or displaying the company logo. In France, Germany and Austria advertising posters are common in schools. In Sweden there are 'branded' curtains in canteens.

Commercial

this covers things like voucher schemes and tokens where schools get equipment based on the number of product tokens collected by pupils and parents, for example Walkers Crisps Books for Schools and Tescos Computers for Schools which raised £60m of IT equipment for schools across the UK and helped Tesco to increase its brand share by 60 per cent. You can see why they did it, a very good 'return on their investment'!'

However, linking fast food and snack food to schools is becoming increasingly unpopular so choose your partners carefully.

Until 2001 a voluntary code of practice existed drawn up by the National Consumer Council on how much branded activity (i.e. advertising a certain company or brand) a school might enter into with a company but a new code of practice has since been developed by the Incorporated Society of British Advertisers (IBA) and the Consumers Association endorsed by the Department for Education and Skills, which provides a framework governing the relationship between commerce and education. The guidelines at www.isba.org.uk cover teaching packs and materials, sponsored activities and collector schemes.

Patronage

this is where individuals or organisations donate money to buy equipment, improve buildings and fund staffing posts; this is more commonly called funding.

Some questions to ask

Wherever you get your funding from (and more about this later) before you dive headlong into fundraising there are some fundamental questions you need to ask.

1 How does fundraising fit into our school's development plan?
2 Can we justify to others and ourselves the reasons for raising extra funds?
3 Do most of the staff and governors support what we are doing?
4 Will the parents and friends support us?

If the answer to all the above is yes then you can proceed.

In summary

- there are plenty of opportunities for schools to raise money but the competition is fierce
- for schools to succeed they need to adopt a professional approach to fundraising
- be prepared for hard work and for it to take time
- view fundraising as an ongoing activity, a fact of school life
- there are four broad areas to fundraising for schools:

Fundraising for your school

**educational
sponsorship
commercial
patronage**

2
What are you fundraising for?

The first rule is to be clear exactly what you are fundraising for. Of course this will change as you journey along your fundraising road but before you embark on this arduous and time-consuming journey be clear exactly *why* you are undertaking it and *what* you would like to achieve. It is important here that you consult the various stakeholders involved with your school, that is staff, parents, governors and possibly pupils.

Why? Because you will surely meet resistance and cynicism from those around you and sometimes it is difficult enough to keep going when you meet rejections without adding to it the hostility and apathy of others. Of course it is not possible to win over everyone, but at least by involving others you are giving them the opportunity to participate (so they can't accuse you later of not involving them) and you could also win some converts along the way.

How to persuade the sceptics

It will probably be impossible to persuade every member of your staff to your way of thinking, not to mention winning over all your governors and parents, and you could expend a great deal of time and energy trying. First then, it is important to identify those staff members who are committed to fundraising, or could easily be persuaded to the idea of fundraising. These can often be staff who are going to benefit most directly. For example if you are raising funds for a new music room then the music teacher is going to be an obvious ally.

It is also wise to identify the reasons for the staffs' resistance to fundraising and these can often be genuine concerns like, how much more time is going to be demanded from me? What am I going to be asked to do? Do I have the necessary skills to become involved? And from these questions, which are often rooted in fear, comes the other statement often heard, 'Fundraising isn't part of my role as a teacher', or variations on this theme.

So before you start to sell the idea to all your staff, parents and governors – and yes, you do have to sell it – you need to have thoroughly thought through your ideas, be prepared for how you are going to present the initial concept and how you are going to answer objections.

Here are some tips on how to approach this.

Identify those members of staff who are most likely to be your allies; one or two could be enough to start with. Get them fully on your side and thrash out your ideas with them. These people could form the basis of your fundraising committee (see Chapter 4).

What are you fundraising for?

Alternatively you can do this with your Senior Management Team and identify which of them are likely to be your best allies – hopefully they all will but be prepared for the sceptics.

Identify with these allies the type of objections that you will meet from the staff and work out how you are going to answer these.

Understand the fundraising process and what is involved, not necessarily the nitty gritty but the broad outlines so that you can respond to the objections. Read this book before approaching your staff and you will have the rudiments of the fundraising process under your belt. Enrol on a course, talk to other schools that have been successful in this; how did they go about their fundraising?

Once you are happy to proceed, introduce the subject of fundraising to the whole school staff perhaps by way of giving a presentation or a series of presentations. Answer any questions they may have and then charge them with going away and in their teams/groups identifying areas that they would like to raise funds for i.e. a wish list, ideas on fundraising and what they can do if anything to help. If they come up with more questions or objections then fine, welcome them and make a point of answering them as best you can. The more you can involve them the greater their commitment.

Be enthusiastic about your fundraising. Ask your allies to be enthusiastic and to lobby others within the school for support as you progress with your fundraising.

Fundraising is a long, slow haul and the greatest disillusionment comes in the early stages when people seem to be doing a great deal for very little result. Once people see some tangible benefits, for example new equipment or project funding, you will win more support.

Your wish list

> Before you ask them for their ideas and wish list urge them to think BIG.

If you are going to put in all this effort to raise funds then there is no point doing it for small amounts of money. If you are really serious about generating additional funds and an additional income for your school, then you need to approach the whole thing as a professional and be committed to it for the long haul. Get rid of the 'well we could always buy the cheapest equipment' or 'second hand will do.' It will not do: you want the best for your school and you have good reasons to want the best.

So tell them to be imaginative, no holds barred. If they had unlimited money what would they want. Don't shout anyone down and don't laugh at them or tell them what they wish for is impossible – it may not be.

Once you have your wish list take a good hard look at it. Can some of these projects be rolled up together? Are they all fundable from outside sources or should statutory funding really finance some of them? For example on your list might be a new staff room, or a new classroom, or more storage area. None of these are going to be very attractive to external funders but it is possible that your re-development scheme which includes providing a new library, music room and access room for adult classes could also encompass that new staff room or classroom.

Can you group together any of the items you require under headings? For example the new music room and all the new music room equipment would go under one heading and it might be that you need new staging, movable seating and lighting for the hall. All this could be wrapped up into one appeal under the heading of new Drama and Music suite.

Example wish list

School newsletter

School brochure

School play/performances

Outings

Prizes

Minibus

School playground and ground redesign

School playground equipment

Environmental garden

ICT suite (new classroom)

ICT equipment

Electronic white boards

Networked computers to all classrooms

Laptops

Staging for hall

Removable seating for hall

Lighting

Music equipment

Sports hall

Sports equipment

Swimming pool refurbishment

Changing rooms

Put a cost against each item

Once you have your wish list you need to get an idea of how much each item will cost. Also obtain estimates from builders for any building or refurbishment work. You will also need to get drawings from architects. Don't forget to build in a cost for inflation.

For things like the school newsletter and brochure, work out how much it costs you to produce these now and, if you could improve them and be more lavish, how much that would cost.

Assign a cost to each item in your wish list and then add it all up. This is your total **appeal target**. This is not set in stone, it will change just as Priory's did (they started with £1 million and ended up with an appeal figure of £2.5 million).

Follow the example of other charitable organizations; they launch their appeals always with a target financial figure and with details of what they hope to achieve by raising that money.

Allocate a time scale

Now divide a piece of paper up into three columns under the headings, short term, medium term and long term.

Short term

This is what you can achieve within a term. Generally it is the smaller items on your list and those that require sponsorship. For example from our wish list it would be sponsoring the School newsletter, or brochures, prizes at prize-giving and supporting the play.

Medium term

This is what you can achieve by the end of the school year so generally this is the more expensive items from our list; it could possibly be the environmental garden and the purchase of some equipment.

Long term

This includes those items and capital build projects that will take you more than a year to raise funds for.

> Now taking the items on your own wish list put them under three headings.

Not only does this help when organizing your fundraising (see Chapter 3) but it also helps you to identify the potential sources of funding, (see below and Chapters 6, 7, 8 and 9).

Potential funders and time scales

Potential funders include:
- small local companies
- local branches of national companies
- large multinationals
- trusts and foundations
- grants – local, national and european
- Lottery grants
- local community
- parents
- pupils
- past pupils
- PTA or Friends of the School
- suppliers and potential suppliers
- high wealth individuals
- celebrities

Different funders have different processes. From a quick glance at the above list you can see that it will take you longer to raise money from a grant application than it would say from a pupil or parent. A grant application will also be higher in value than a contribution from a parent. So let's return now to our three columns – short term, medium term and long term and identify the potential funders under these three headings.

Short term
local companies
local branches of national companies
pupils
parents
PTA
local community

Medium term
large multinational companies
local companies
local branches of national companies
parents
pupils
past pupils
local community
PTA

Long term
trusts and foundations
grants including Lottery
large multinational corporates
local community

Before we look at how we find these potential funders it is important that you organize yourselves for fundraising in the most efficient manner.

In summary

- be clear what you are fundraising for
- consult the various stakeholders for their ideas and draw up a wish list
- identify those staff members, parents and governors who are committed to fundraising
- identify the type of objections to fundraising you are likely to meet from staff, parents and governors
- give a presentation or series of presentations to the staff, answer any questions and address their concerns
- put a cost against each item on your wish list, get builders' estimates and architect's drawings
- add it all up to give you your total appeal figure
- allocate a time scale to your funding
    short term
    medium term
    long term

3
Organizing for fundraising

As you have already gathered from reading the previous chapters, and by looking at your wish list, there is a lot of work to be done and no one person can do it by her or himself. You will need help. So what are the options open to you?

Engage an external fundraiser or fundraising organization

There are many professional fundraisers and organizations around who can help you but obviously they will cost. But then all fundraising will cost, whether you do it yourself or enlist outside help. The time you and your staff spend fundraising takes you and them away from the jobs they are employed to do and therefore carries a cost. But if you decide to engage a professional organization to help, be clear about the costs this involves and budget accordingly. Very few if any professional fundraisers now work on a commission-only basis but are much more likely to work on an hourly rate basis which could range from £40 per hour to £140 per hour! So be clear about their charges before engaging them.

You must also be clear exactly what you want them to do. They can often help you kick-start your project and do the initial work, or perhaps you will engage a specialist organization to conduct telephone campaigns or to organize some major fundraising events. I have listed below some areas where a professional fundraising organization can help you; it is by no means exhaustive. You may wish to return to this section once you have read the rest of the book.

A professional fundraising organization can:

- conduct your brain storming wish list activity
- research and put together the appeal
- research potential funders on your behalf
- contact and meet with potential funders
- organize fundraising events
- handle fundraising media coverage
- advise you on how to set up a charity and make sure you adhere to all the relevant legal requirements
- help keep you on track with your fundraising by meeting with you regularly.

> You could engage a professional fundraising agency for all or part of the project or for a specific time.

Ask who will be working on your account, what experience do they have personally of working with schools and does the agency have of fundraising for schools. It is important to ask this and to choose a fundraiser who understands the way schools work and the fundraising issues that surround them, which are different to other charitable causes. When trying to find a suitable agency to engage ask around your colleagues from other schools to see if they can recommend anyone or contact the Institute of Fundraising at www.institute-of-fundraising.org.uk. This site not only gives a directory of consultants but also provides other updates and guidance on fundraising as well as latest conferences and events, some aimed at schools.

Employ a fundraiser

Some of the larger schools I know have gone down the road of employing a professional fundraiser within the school either full time or part time. Sometimes this person is referred to as a Development or Commercial Director. If you do decide to appoint someone internally you are looking at a senior position, someone who can work alongside the head teacher. You would certainly be looking at paying that person the equivalent of a deputy head teacher's salary. He or she would be expected, over a period of time, to generate enough income to pay for his salary as well as generate the required funds for the school. But don't expect great things too quickly and this is where the element of risk comes in. You may be paying out money on a salary, as well as giving this person the space and equipment (computer/telephone etc.) to work and see nothing for your money for the first year.

Again, like our professional fundraising agency, it is ideal if the candidate has experience of fundraising for schools although not essential. What is important is that they have a proven track record of raising funds and know how to approach various funders. If you decide to go down this road then at least by reading this book you will have a better understanding of what to expect from them and hopefully at the interview stage ask the right questions.

Some schools have joined together in their fundraising efforts and have appointed a fund raising professional to work on their behalf.

Do it yourself

As I have already said it is very difficult, in fact nigh on impossible, to do it all yourself; you will need help so it is a good idea to set up a small but very active and willing committee to help you. There are a number of ways you can divide the tasks of the committee members.

For example, you may appoint someone on the committee to raise funds from the rich and famous, another to concentrate on Trust fundraising and another to concentrate on business – both local and corporate, with someone else responsible for fundraising and liaising with the community and parents.

Alternatively, you may decide to divide up the wish list and allocate fundraising projects but this leaves more room for duplication as one person fundraising for, say, playground equipment could approach the same potential funder as the person who is fundraising for staging and lighting for the hall. However you allocate the tasks, regular communication is absolutely essential – as is the fact that everyone must pull their weight.

The committee structure works very well for some schools but is disastrous for others.

Appoint one person to fundraise from within the school

In some schools a teacher is pulled away from teaching full-time and given the task of fundraising, reporting directly to the head teacher. This has worked successfully for some schools I know but it depends greatly on the person fundraising, their willingness, interpersonal skills and organizing ability.

With Priory School I worked closely on an ongoing basis with the deputy head teacher who was instrumental in driving the project forward and helping to secure funding and who would from time to time enlist other teachers help. With Willows, a special school, I worked with the head teacher and a small but very dedicated committee which also included the deputy head teacher.

With Isambard Brunel Junior School I held an initial three-hour meeting with a small committee which included the head teacher. They were then charged with going away and doing their research and we reconvened a couple of months later when I checked they had covered all the areas they needed and then set them off in the right direction. This small working party or committee still meets once a fortnight and comprises the community site manager, office manager, the head teacher and a teacher, who has since become the community link teacher working three days a week.

The school has done very well indeed raising £300,000 from various grants and has become the lead extended school in the area.

However you decide to organize yourself for fundraising, there is one thing you definitely need and that is a head teacher who is committed to and enthusiastic about fundraising. Ideally it helps if he or she has one or two others on board!

In summary

- different funders have different application procedures and some take longer than others to raise money from
- it is important that you organize yourselves for fundraising in the most efficient manner
- there are a number of ways you can organize yourself for fundraising:
- engage the services of a fundraising agency;
- appoint a professional fundraiser either part-time or full-time;
- do it yourself – appoint a small but active fundraising committee;
- appoint someone from within the school to be responsible for fundraising
- the head teacher needs to be enthusiastic about fundraising.

4
Registering as a charity

OK so you've decided how you should be organized and formed a small committee to help you progress this exciting venture for your school but there are more questions that need to be settled before you get down to the nitty gritty of fundraising.

Do we need to register as a charity?

It is not strictly necessary to register with the Charity Commission (see www.charity-commission.gov.uk) but it might help you to unlock funding from various sources, primarily Trusts and Foundations and some Corporations who state that they will only give to registered charities.

It really depends on how ambitious your project is and how much money you need to raise. You should also consider whether you are into fundraising long-term or just to meet a short-term priority. If you are only seeking to raise a small amount of money, or you are looking for sponsorship of, say, your newsletter, to fund outings, or for small items of equipment, then it will probably not be worth the effort of registering as a charity with the Charities Commission. If, however, you are considering raising funds as a long-term strategy as part of your school's development plan, which could include substantial amounts of money, then yes it is worthwhile.

Trusts, Foundations and Corporations are not in the business of giving money for what they consider should be fulfilled by 'statutory' funding. If you make an application for funding on your school letterhead then it could get rejected at the first hurdle. If you make an application on your registered charity letterhead, giving the charity registration number and demonstrating that your scheme is well thought out, well planned and targeted, then you will at least get considered.

Many schools already have registered charities. This is often the PTA, or Friends of the School and you may wish to fundraise under this umbrella. Your decision could be based on what role the PTA/Friends plays in your school and what they fundraise for. Some schools prefer to leave the PTA to continue with low level/local or short-term fundraising with the power to direct the funds they raise as they see fit, and set up another charity to raise funds for larger projects including capital build.

In addition, under Gift Aid any payment made to a school charity by any taxpayer is eligible for tax relief providing that you supply the donor with a Gift Aid declaration form, and providing that you record each donation separately so that you can demonstrate to the Inland Revenue how much each donor has given.

So the arguments for registering or not must be considered and again once you have read this book you may have a clearer idea of whether or not it is appropriate for your school. If you decide that it is appropriate then you would be advised to visit the Charities Commission web site for further details and information which will guide you through the process. It is not that painful but it will take time.

Do I need a separate bank account for fundraising?

If you are a registered charity, or decide to set up a registered charity, then the answer is yes you will need to open a separate bank account in the registered charity name. If you hold school voluntary funds on trust then you need to be accountable for these to whichever body is appropriate. In the case of a registered charity this is the Charities Commission. All charities are required to maintain accounting records (which must be retained for at least six years), to prepare accounts, and to make the accounts available to the public on request, although you can make a reasonable charge for photocopying and administration. There are various different requirements for charities depending on their level of income and for full details it is best to obtain the relevant publications available from the Charities Commission.

When choosing a bank account it is advisable to investigate the various benefits offered by those institutions, for example the rates of interest offered, the timing of interest payments, the conditions of access to money including whether or not there is access at short notice without penalty, and whether interest is paid gross or net of tax. Non-financial considerations such as personal service and the location of the bank are also important but less so than those mentioned above.

Appointing trustees and/or committee members

If you decide to register as a charity then you will need to appoint trustees. If you decide against this you will still need a small committee of people to help you fundraise. The criteria for becoming a trustee are listed in the following pages, and these could equally apply to committee members.

Becoming a trustee of a charity is not something to embark upon lightly or for the sake of looking good on a CV, and although some people do become trustees purely for this reason, they should also be made fully aware of the responsibilities it entails.

Trustees must be willing to pull their weight and to become active members of your charitable organisation. You cannot afford to have trustees who only turn up at the meetings and then disappear again, contributing little or nothing to advancing your charitable cause. As well as appointing individuals who are fully aware of their duties, and who take them seriously, you also want a team who can work together.

> For any team to be effective you need a variety of skills and personalities, a mix of people all able to work together for the common purpose, in this case successful fundraising.

Finance

This person will be responsible for overseeing that all charity bank accounts are operated correctly (e.g. by more than one person), that funds held for different purposes are kept in separate bank accounts and that the charity's accounting records accurately reflect the movement of funds.

They must ensure that the charity's money is spent solely for the purposes set out in the charity's governing document. In addition, the finance trustee must ensure that the charity avoids speculation, invests prudently and monitors the performance of investments made on behalf of the charity, conforming to the Trustee Act 2000.

Legal

This person will ensure that all staff employed by the charity have a proper contract of employment and a written job description making clear the extent of his authority to act on the charity's behalf. They will also ensure that the documentation regarding the recruitment, appointment and resignation of trustees complies with the charity's governing document, the Charity Commission rules and regulations and other employment legislation. Working closely with the other trustees, the legal trustee will ensure that all documentation and charity activity is compliant with legislation and the Charity Commission requirements.

If you decide not to go down the registered charity route then this appointment will not be so necessary or perhaps not required at all. Your staff will or should all have contracts of employment and job descriptions anyway. You may find that you have a governor with legal expertise who can join your fundraising committee or alternatively the local authority legal representatives can handle any legal questions.

For certain fundraising activities it is best to check out the legal position, this can apply to things like street collections and lotteries (see Chapter 14).

Marketing

If possible have someone on your committee, or as a trustee, who has some marketing and/or media experience. This could help you when discussing fundraising ideas and raising your profile through the media (see Chapter 13).

Secretarial

This trustee or committee member is ideally someone who is good at minute taking, organized and efficient and who can photocopy and circulate minutes to the trustees in advance of the meetings. This person can also arrange the meetings, check the venue and brief the Chairman on agenda items as well as contributing to the meeting.

Chairman

The Chairman will be responsible for overseeing the meetings, keeping the meeting to order and agenda items, also extracting contributions from each member, debating points within the time frame, agreeing action and ensuring this is minuted and carried out.

It is important to note that decisions concerning the charity are taken by the trustees acting together and no one person. However, you will be able to ask certain people to look into particular matters connected with the charity and to make recommendations, but the decision whether or not to act on the recommendations is for the trustees to take together. No single trustee should be allocated a part of the income of a charity or expected to manage any particular aspect alone. According to your governing document you may permit the trustees to set up committees with limited powers to carry out particular functions.

In addition to these key positions trustees (or committee members) should be passionate about your cause, not afraid of hard work, willing to contribute ideas, roll up their sleeves and muck in and for no financial reward other than knowing they are helping their school and community.

Full details on becoming a Trustee can be obtained by contacting the Charity Commission or visiting www.charity-commission.gov.uk.

As you can see Trusteeship of a charity and committee membership is not something to be entered into lightly.

In summary

- it is not strictly necessary to register as a charity – it depends on how ambitious your fundraising project is and whether or not you are in it for the long term or short term
- the PTA or Friends are often already registered as a charity and you may wish to fundraise under

their umbrella

- Trusts and Foundations and some companies will only give to registered charities
- choose your Trustees or Committee members carefully, they should be committed to your cause and enthusiastic
- ideally have trustees who have marketing, legal and financial experience, and you will also need a secretary and a chairperson.

5
Preparation and writing your appeal

Once you have got your basic structure right and know what you are fundraising for and how much money you would like to raise, it is time to start putting together all the information that prospective funders will require.

> You need to make your case for funding as strongly as possible.

This information is pulled together in an Appeal Document (sometimes referred to as a Business Plan).

> Many schools fail in their applications for funding because they have failed to do their preparation.

I know this is time consuming and rather irritating because you'd much rather get on with the real business but be patient: by conducting your research and pulling it all together in one document you will save yourself a great deal of time in the long run and have more success.

If, however, you are only fundraising for small items, or trying to obtain sponsorship for the school newsletter, play, outings, prizes etc. i.e. short-term funding, then there will probably be no need to prepare an appeal document. It will be unlikely that you will be applying to Trusts and Foundations, or for grants or for large sums of money from businesses and the rich and famous. If fundraising solely from businesses both large and small in your locality then you will need to read Chapters 9, 10, 11 and 12.

But anyone who is looking at securing substantial funding from medium and long-term sources will need to make their case and hence will need an Appeal Document or Business Plan of some kind.

Researching

So, you may be asking, what exactly goes into this Appeal Document? The answer – anything that can help you make your case for funding.

Your research needs to answer the questions:

- why do we need funding?
- what are we fundraising for?
- who does it involve?
- what sort of evidence do we have to back this up? (For example have you identified a need in your

Preparation and writing your appeal

area for the facilities/equipment/resources you require funding for?
- what is the nature of the problem we are tackling?
- what will providing this funding do to help the children, parents and community?
- who will use the new facilities?
- what difference will it make to the people who live in our area?

To answer these questions you will need some if not all of the following information:

- population statistics for your area
- breakdown by age, employment, housing and health, ethnicity – anything in fact that supports your case for funding
- social trends
- socio-economic details about the people who live and work in your area
- index of multiple deprivation – which can be found at the neighbourhood statistics services, www.neighbourhood.statistics.gov.uk
- possibly public transport or car ownership information, for example your school may be in a rural area which is poorly served by public transport and by increasing your facilities you are providing a much needed local service to the community, you are helping to keep teenagers off the streets and out of trouble.
- existing facilities in your area – for example you may wish to provide a new sports facility or drama studio, or health and fitness suite. What already

exists in the area, how much do they charge? Are you offering something different, better or more affordable?

Much of this research can be gleaned from your local council's web site. In addition, check out with the local council their Strategic Plans and obtain a copy of these. Talk to the relevant contacts at the council and tell them what you intend doing, see if you can work together – you might be able to help them to fulfil part of their strategic plan by providing the new facility. You never know, you might even get funding from them! You will certainly need their support and if you can demonstrate that you have this, this will greatly enhance your chances of winning funding from Trusts and Foundations and other grant-giving bodies.

Another useful source of information is the National Statistics Office. Visit their web site www.statistics.gov.uk. It really makes fascinating reading as does their quarterly magazine *Horizons* which you can subscribe to free of charge.

You will need to liaise with other organisations, both voluntary and state-funded, for example the Primary Health Care Trusts on health issues, or Help the Aged if your project involves the older members of the local population. All these organisations will have conducted their own research at some time and have access to government statistics.

You may also need to conduct your own surveys or consultations to ascertain if there is a need in your area for what you are proposing. Contact existing voluntary and state bodies to see if they have already consulted with the local population and if so, what were the results of that consultation. Explore whether or not there is any scope for you to work together.

Give your appeal a name

Your charitable appeal will need branding, i.e. an identity, something that people can remember and become familiar with. This is based on the marketing principle that people buy what they are familiar with and you need them to buy into your cause.

For example:

Priory School's £2.5 million appeal was called the CAN DO appeal. CAN DO actually stood for Community, Achieving, New Developments and Opportunities.

Willows Nursery School Appeal was called the SKIP appeal, which stood for Special Kids in Portsmouth.

Involve all your stakeholders in coming up with a catchy and imaginative name for your appeal. This also separates it from the PTA fundraising.

You will also need to devise a logo, rather than using your school logo. Here you can engage the pupils if you wish, or a design agency or designer might tackle this for you free of charge as their way of sponsoring you.

This appeal name and logo, along with your charity registration number, will go on your letterhead and it is this letterhead that you will mail out rather than the school letterhead. Why? Because as I mentioned before, some trusts and foundations and businesses will not fund schools and if they receive an application on a school letterhead, even though your cause is a good one, they could bin it straight away.

Writing the appeal

Write your appeal document on a computer so that sections of it can be copied and pasted and adapted to suit different funders. Do not produce an expensive glossy brochure, which would not only cost you a fortune but could also be out of date the moment it is printed. In addition, if potential funders receive an expensive glossy brochure from you they will ask if you really need the money. A small leaflet outlining in broad terms your fundraising appeal, with a reply section, is acceptable and indeed helpful as you will talk to many people about your fundraising appeal and it is useful to give them something to read. You may also wish to keep a stock in reception for parents and other visitors to pick up and take away. Perhaps you can even get this small leaflet sponsored by a local business?

Here is some of the information you will need to put into your Appeal Document:

1 **Our appeal target**
   State how much you wish to raise.

2 **About our appeal**
   Next include a couple of paragraphs which state the:
   aim of the appeal
   your mission/vision

3 **What we require funding for**
   List/describe how that appeal target has been set i.e. what you are fundraising for.

4 **About our school**
   Give some background on your school; the brief history, how many pupils it has, their ages and

background. What is so special about your school? What is special about your pupils?

5 Why we need funding
What is the nature of the problem you are tackling? In effect why are you raising this money? What will it do to help the children, the parents, the wider community? Who will use the new facilities? What difference will it make to the people who live in your area? Include the evidence to support your claim.

6 What are the consequences of the problem if nothing is done?
For example if we have teenagers wandering the streets and getting bored are they more likely to turn to crime? If our cause is to prevent this by providing a much needed facility then we need to back it up with crime figures and surveys; we need to liaise with the police and the youth services and we need to demonstrate that we are working closely with them and have their support.

7 What are your key selling points i.e. why should people fund you?
Boost your credibility here, give endorsements from others who support you or who have funded you in the past. What is your track record? How successful and imaginative have you been in past projects? Just remember no one is going to give you money unless they can trust you to spend it wisely and get results.

Say why you are qualified to run this programme or project.

Include extracts from letters you receive from grateful parents and others, including pupils or students.

Ask experts to visit you and then get them to write to you with their impression of your work. Ask if you can use selected quotes in your Appeal Document.

8 The project itself
Who is it aimed at? Give details of specific programmes, projects etc. How many young people will be helped? How will they use the programme or the facilities? What do the community think about what you are doing? Have you consulted them? If so show survey results.

9 What will be the outcomes of your project?
What will be its impact? How long will it take to measure this impact and just how are you going to measure success?

10 Project planning
Include a project plan with timings, especially if it includes refurbishment work or new build. Provide a budget covering all the items of expenditure you plan to incur plus any income you expect to generate from the project. Include:
  capital costs
  architectural drawings
  equipment
  staffing costs

11 Who else is involved?
Who is on your project committee? What expertise do they have for example in accounts, marketing/PR, project management. What part do the individuals play in the project?

Bring people into your organisation as expert advisers, specialist sub-committees, patrons etc.

Who else is involved in the community? What is

your collaboration with other organisations? Who are your community partners?

12 State how you intend to raise the funds
What is the proportion of funds you have generated or propose to generate through pupil fundraising, from parents and others? State the statutory funding that is being provided, if any.

13 Contact details
Always ensure you have given information on how a potential funder should contact you and preferably include a fax back or reply form in your application to make it easy for people to respond. As it is sometimes difficult to get hold of individuals within schools because of meetings and teaching commitments it is a good idea to provide two contact names and one of those to be contactable most of the time, for example a member of your administration or support staff.

It is rare that the complete Appeal Document or Business Plan will be sent out, certainly not at the first stage of an application, when quite often only a summary or outline, usually about two pages of A4 information, is required. This can be extracted from your main document.

When you come to complete application forms for grants you will already have some, if not all the information you can pull from your master document and drop into the application. If a Trust or Foundation is interested and serious about donating you money then they will want to see the complete plan with cash flow forecasts and financial projections if your project involves developing a facility that involves a fee-paying public.

In summary

- you need to make your case for funding as strongly as possible.
- this information is pulled together in an Appeal Document
- many schools fail in their applications for funding because they have failed to do their preparation
- your research needs to answer the questions:

    Why do we need funding?

    What are we fundraising for?

    Who does it involve?

    What sort of evidence do we have to back this up?

    What is the nature of the problem we are tackling?

    What will providing this funding do to help the children, parents, and community?

    Who will use the new facilities?

    What difference will it make to the people who live in our area?

- much of this research can be gleaned from your local council's web site and other statutory and voluntary bodies
- conduct your own surveys and consult your community
- give your appeal a name to brand it and make it stand out
- devise a logo

- write your Appeal Document on a computer so that sections of it can be copied and pasted and adapted to suit different funders
- your Appeal Document should include:
    the Appeal target;
    about our Appeal;
    what we require funding for;
    about our school;
    why we need funding;
    what are the consequences of the problem if nothing is done?
    our key selling points i.e. why should people fund us?
    the project itself;
    the outcomes of our project;
    project planning;
    who else is involved?
    how we intend to raise the funds;
    contact details.

6
Sources of funding – trusts, foundations and grants

Researching potential funders

Now you are ready to research potential funders. Where do you find the relevant Trusts and Foundations to approach? Where can you get hold of details on wealthy or well-connected patrons? How can you track down the large corporates and other businesses? And what sort of grants are available to you?

This chapter examines information on Trusts, Foundations and Grants while the following chapters provide information on locating and approaching the rich and famous and businesses.

Directory of Social Change

If you haven't already discovered the Directory of Social Change (DSC) then I suggest you start here. This organisation is based in London (near Euston Station) and in Liverpool, Hope Street. The London centre contains a collection of over 100 titles covering information on funding and fundraising; the Liverpool centre fewer titles. But you don't need to go to either London or Liverpool to access the information. The DSC produces a catalogue of books and CD ROMs for purchase.

I suggest you visit their web site at www.dsc.org.uk or obtain a catalogue of their products. You can e-mail them for a copy on books@dsc.org.uk. In their catalogue you will find a complete section on fundraising, which includes books and CD ROMs on grant-making trusts, companies, Government and EU grants and details on overseas grant makers.

One such CD ROM is **Grant Making Trusts**. This combines the Trusts databases of the Directory of Social Change and the Charities Aid Foundation. It is updated annually and gives information on 4,000 UK grant-making trusts giving over £1 billion a year. You can search by geographical area to identify trusts in your region, by the type of activity that they award grants to, for example arts, sports etc. or by trust name, trustee or type of grant. It provides contact details and information on how to apply to the Trust or Foundation.

The software is available in PC format only and can be run on Windows 95 upwards. It can also be networked and there is a tutorial feature to help you get started.

If you don't wish to go down the route of having the CD ROM then you can access the information via a website www.trustfunding.org.uk. This provides all the same information as the CD ROM but is updated throughout the year. Subscribers are alerted to updates via e-mail.

You may also like to check with your local library or local education authority as they may hold this CD ROM and other information I have listed, which you might be able to access for free.

Contact details for the Directory of Social Change are:
DSC
24 Stephenson Way
London
NW1 2DP
Tel: 020 7209 5151
e-mail: books@dsc.org.uk
web site: www.dsc.org.uk

Profunding

Profunding provides an online service to help fundraisers. The web site www.fundinginformation.org was launched in 1998 and gives information and coverage on funding issues and hot topics as well as details of grants, including European grants. Once registered as a user you receive a personal ID and password that allows you access to the site. In addition users are sent an e-mail alert whenever the site is updated.

There are sections for each of the major fund sources, grants from Trusts, Companies, Government and Europe as well as information about attracting funding from individual donors. These can be printed out, or, at the end of the month, can be downloaded in one file. The site is broken into three areas:

Getting money

Sources of money include: Lottery, Europe, central and local government, advanced details of newly registered grant-making trusts and individual donors.

Future trends

This tells you about the political, economic, social and technological forces that shape fundraising practices in the future.

More effective fundraising

This brings you details on courses, conferences and publications.

Contact details are:
Profunding
Suite 1.02
St Mary's Centre
Oystershell Lane
Newcastle upon Tyne
NE4 5QS
tel: 0191 232 6942
fax: 0191 232 6936
e-mail: info@fundinginformation.org.
www.fundinginformation.org

Funderfinder

Funderfinder produces two software packages for the fundraiser: People in Need (PIN) and Groups in Need (GIN).

People in Need (PIN) is a programme that identifies charitable funds that could help a person in need, for example if they need assistance with nursing home fees or some equipment to make their life more bearable.

Groups in Need (GIN) is of more relevance to schools; it can help to identify sources of funding from over 4,500 potential funders including Trusts and Foundations. A search provides a list of funders which can be saved, exported and printed.

More information can be obtained on this by visiting the company's web site at www.funderfinder.org.uk.

Grantfinder

Grantfinder is available on the Internet or CD ROM. *Grantfinder* provides details on grants, subsidies, loans, venture funding and other incentives available not just to the voluntary sector but also to businesses, some 1,900 in total. It also includes details on grants and schemes available through the DTI, DETR and Dfee, Employment Service, European Commission and other schemes applicable to the UK. You can print off a one-page summary of each scheme with its purpose, criteria, main contact point and details.

It is worth checking with your local council to see if they are already subscribing to it and if so whether you can have access to the information via them. In Hampshire, for example, the Pompey Study Centre in Portsmouth makes access to this database freely available to any school.

Contact details are:
Grantfinder
Enterprise House
Carlton Road
Worksop

Nottinghamshire S81 7QF
tel: 01909 501200
e-mail: enquiries@grantfinder.co.uk
web site: www.grantfinder.co.uk

Who's Who in Charities

This provides up to date biographies on 50,000 charity patrons and trustees. It gives information on the Top 1500 Corporate Donors with details of the most generous UK companies, how much they give and who to contact. It can help provide information and contacts especially useful when making a grant application.

Available in book or CD format there is a single- user or multi-user licence. You can search by name, education, professional and recreational interest, print off lists and build your own list. There is also a mail merge facility.

Contact details are:
CaritasData Limited
Paulton House
8 Shepherdess Walk
London
N1 7LB
tel: 0207 566 8210
web site: www.caritasdata.com

Fundraising tips

If it's fundraising tips you want then *First Monday* provide some very useful fundraising tips on the first Monday of every month by e-mail. They also provide more detailed tips and funding information through their Monthly Fundraising Newsletter which is sent by e-mail.

To subscribe send a blank e-mail message to firstmonday-on@list.drfgroup.co.uk.

Contact details:
DRF Group Limited
2440 The Quadrant
Aztec West
Almondsbury
Bristol BS32 4AQ
Tel: 01454 878 573
Fax: 01454 878 673

Practical Funding for Schools

Then there is an excellent publication called *Practical Funding for Schools*. This not only gives useful tips and articles on fundraising but also provides case studies from schools that have been successful in raising money. In addition it includes an extremely useful round up on grants. It is produced monthly and to subscribe contact 01926 420046 or visit www.practicalfunding.com

Raising money from trusts and foundations

So how do you identify the appropriate trusts and foundations to target?

Using one of the sources mentioned in the previous pages conduct a search to see what each Trust and Foundation or grant-giving body will fund. This will usually be stated, for example: education, older people, animal based projects, environmental projects, medical research etc. Some may state quite clearly that they do not fund schools. If however your project involves the community then you may wish to contact them to see if it is worthwhile putting in an application. Some will also state that they only consider applications from within a geographical area, for example: London or the South West or Newcastle etc. If your project does not fit their criteria then don't waste your time and theirs by applying.

In addition look at what they have actually funded (this is also often stated in the details) as this can give you clues as to your chances of securing funding. They will give you clear directions on how to apply for funding, so follow their procedures religiously. If they state you must apply on their application form then telephone and obtain one. If they state they want a two-page proposal then give them two pages and not four.

You will also need to look at when they will accept an application as there might be a specific time period for this, so check if you have missed the deadline and if so make a diary note for the following year and apply then.

If you are uncertain about any of the information or the application criteria then you can always telephone the Trust and obtain the information; generally speaking the people who work for Trusts and Foundations are extremely helpful and friendly. Here is a list of some things you might like to ask them.

- the date of the next trustees meeting so that you have an idea of when they might be considering your application
- any recent changes to policy or priorities to ensure it is worth your while applying

- the usual level and type of donation
- the frequency of donations
- the amount of information needed in the application if it has not been stated.

When examining the information about the Trust review the Board of Trustees to see if there is anyone known to you, or likely to be known to a staff member or a parent – a personal letter or a letter signed by someone known has a far greater chance of success.

Prepare your proposal, taking the relevant information from your Appeal Document, tailoring this for the individual application where appropriate. Send in the application but be very careful that you have done your research well and that you have adhered to all of the stated requirements. If you get it wrong, or put in a slap dash application, you will have blown your chances of reapplying for at least another year and maybe two as many Trusts specify when you can reapply and how many times you can make an application. The general rule is three strikes and you're out.

Writing the appeal letter

This will accompany your application. It will be no longer than one-and-a-half sides of A4. It encapsulates the essence of your Appeal and your application to that Trust, Foundation or grant-giving body. It should be personally addressed to a named person, hand signed and tailored to that particular organisation's requirements. It should not appear to be a general mail-out sent around to everyone. To provide you with a guideline of what it should contain here is an example letter.

Dear «salutation»

ABC Special School – ABC Appeal

ABC is a special needs school for children aged 5-8 years who come from all over the City of Anytown. It has an outreach service, which helps families and other people working with young children in the City. Currently it is the only Special Needs School in the UK, which is both an Early Excellence Centre and a Beacon School. It was awarded the Chartermark in February 1999 and is an Investor in People.

Our children have a wide range of problems, for example in talking and understanding, behaving, hearing, seeing and walking. Children may have difficulties such as:

- Hearing and/or visual impairments
- Moderate or severe learning difficulties
- Autistic Spectrum disorders
- Language disorders or delays
- Behavioural problems
- Social deprivation
- Chromosomal disorders

We are seeking to raise the outstanding amount of £300,000 needed to reach our £1.3 million target which will extend the facilities we provide for our children with special needs and their families, and enable us to give more practical support to families and also to increase numbers of children we can help.

Our capital build project includes developing the following:

- Library and outreach room with computers and Internet access
- Music Room
- Language Room
- Home corner
- Training room and Drop In Centre
- Sensory Room
- Ball Room
- Play House
- External Play Area

Anytown is one of the most densely urbanised cities in the United Kingdom and in Europe with a high level of social deprivation. Many of our children come from backgrounds where poverty and lack of opportunity are prevalent.

Sources of funding: trusts, foundations, grants

Why we need funding

In 1975 ABC was built to accommodate just 30 children. Now there are 80 on our school role so conditions are extremely cramped. We are seeking to expand and redevelop our building which will allow children's skills and life chances to be improved, with better facilities for all the children, flexibility in the time children may spend with us and extend our support services to parents, professionals and others. At present children leave aged 8 and may stay for an extra year in exceptional circumstances. Our plans will allow us to extend this – greatly benefiting children with speech and language disorders.

Our track record and targets – how we measure success

We have an excellent record of children entering mainstream school. A 14-year average shows us that 58% enter mainstream education and 38% need special schools and units. Further time at ABC will help to increase this success rate, represent significant savings to the Government, provide better opportunities for young children and improve their opportunity to play a more effective role in society.

We work with our colleagues in Health, Social Services and voluntary organisations to identify and help families and children at risk, provide supervised access visits, assist dysfunctional families, give advice and support parents with multiple births, help those with post-natal depression and provide constructive play strategies. We also support and work with child minders, playgroup workers, children and families in the Sure Start area, staff of Breakfast and After School clubs and staff in infant and junior schools in Anytown.

To date we have raised or have pledged £1,000,000. We now need to raise a further £300,000 to complete the project. Phase one building work begins in August 2004, phase two in March 2005 with completion scheduled for July 2005. Fitting out the interior and equipment will take place in August 2005 with final completion planned for September 2005.

We write to seek the support of your Trustees to assist with funding some of the aspects of this capital build project or the equipment. I attach further details on the ABC Appeal. We would be happy to invite you to our special school to see for yourself the work we undertake and our current conditions.

I thank you for taking the time to read and consider this application and if you need further information, or would like to arrange a visit, please do not hesitate to contact me.

Yours sincerely,

Chair ABC Appeal

Telephone: 023 9212 3456 Registered Charity number: 123456

> Be methodical, plan a manageable programme of approaches and keep records.

Follow up applications with a telephone call by all means but first check your details for when the Trustees meet and give them time to consider your application.

Be prepared for a long, slow process and to spend a considerable amount of time and effort.

In summary

- sources of funding on trusts, foundations and grants are:
    grant-making trusts
    Profunding
    Funderfinder
    Grantfinder
    Who's Who in Charities
    First Monday
    Practical Funding for Schools
- conduct your research carefully; only apply if you meet the criteria of the trust and foundation or grant-giving body
- if in doubt check it out, telephone to get further information
- give them only what they say they require
- don't put in a slap dash application – it will get

thrown out and blow your chances of reapplying for one or two years
- be methodical, keep records and keep looking out for new trusts and applying.

7
Sources of funding – magazines and newspapers

Newspapers and magazines can provide a valuable source of information on potential funders. It doesn't necessarily mean that you have to buy every publication in creation (which would cost you a fortune) or that you personally need to read each one (which would take you forever, and probably either depress you or bore you silly) but if you ask around your staff, your governors, your parents you will probably find that a whole variety of publications are read, from local to national newspapers, broadsheet to tabloid; from special interest magazines to professional and consumer publications, and all can be valuable because all, at some time or another, carry features on business people, celebrities and personalities, as well as information on their charities and interests.

Carry out a survey of who reads what

So, first carry out a survey of who reads what: ask your staff and governors, the PTA and other parents who are involved in the school. These people will be your eyes (readers). Make a list of the publications they read. It doesn't matter if you only start with a few people, hopefully you can build on this over a period of time.

Train your readers to look for relevant articles

Having drawn up your list you need to train your readers to look out for articles and profiles on people, to cut these out and hand them over to you, or to the person you have designated to help you with your fundraising. The sort of thing your readers should be looking for are profiles on business people, sports personalities, celebrities, etc.

Here are some examples. My local newspaper publishes a Business Section ever Tuesday. In this they run an article called Business Profile, picking an eminent businessperson from the locality to talk about his or her business. This also includes a boxed-out profile providing information on his/her first job, school, hobbies etc.

The *Sunday Times* carries similar styled interviews in both the Business Section and in the News Review. In the Business Section, again the interview carries a boxed-out profile called 'Vital Statistics' giving details on where that person went to school, their hobbies and interests etc. Also in The *Sunday Times* Business Section there is a regular feature on 'How I made it', providing valuable information on a businessperson.

The *Daily Telegraph* has a regular Business Interview in its Saturday edition and in its Parent and Education

Section it runs a feature on 'The Teacher who Inspired ...' Jo Brand mentioned a Latin teacher who had inspired her when she attended Tunbridge Wells Grammar School for Girls. Now if I was the head teacher I would be writing to Jo Brand to say how delighted I was to learn that Miss X had inspired her and tell her all about our fundraising appeal.

While assisting one school with their fundraising I read an article in the *Daily Telegraph* about the retiring Chief Executive of a large national Building Society who had been educated in that school's town, but not at that school. He had an academic background in science and we were, at the time, trying to raise money for science labs. We contacted him and, although he said he no longer had any interests or family in the town, he was happy to write a cheque, which he duly did.

Magazines often carry profiles of people. Women's magazines, the Sunday supplements and the gossip magazines like *Hello* all carry celebrity stories. These can also give you information on the celebrity's pet loves and hates, his or her interests and charitable involvements. Yachting magazines carry profiles on business people or celebrities who enjoy sailing, likewise golfers and golfing magazines, and so on ... Wherever there is a profile, or even a news story about someone, read it and see if there is a connection with your school, locality or area of fundraising.

Identifying a connection

Does that person come from your town, city or county? If they do perhaps they attended your school, and even if they didn't, don't worry, the connection is that they lived in your area in the past, or that they are living there now. But if neither of these applies have they mentioned their special interest – is this the same as your fundraising project? For example, if they are a keen tennis player and you are trying to raise money to build tennis courts, then there is a connection. Or perhaps their special hobby is art, or music and you are trying to raise money for these endeavours. Alternatively, they may have mentioned in their article that they have a special interest in helping young people, or have a criticism of young people that you disagree with, perhaps you can demonstrate how you are overcoming these problems through some innovative project that you are trying to raise funds for.

Other sources of useful information include: The *Sunday Times* Rich list, The *Sunday Times* Top 50 Philanthropists, and The *Sunday Times* Fast Track 100. Is there anyone among these who has a connection with your school or your area? Do they have a particular interest in your type of fundraising project?

The business pages of the broadsheets are also worth scanning for articles on entrepreneurs who have sold their businesses. Not all of these newly rich will keep the full proceeds of the sale of their businesses but will set up new Trust Funds to donate to charitable causes; for example businessman and entrepreneur Peter Harrison donated a vast sum of money from the sale of his business to set up the Peter Harrison Foundation. Getting in early could mean you have a better chance of receiving a grant from them. I did just this for Priory School and the school received a cheque for £50,000 towards a new ICT suite.

How to approach them

Once you have the connection (however tenuous) the next step is to contact that person, preferably by telephone, or write to them. If you can't find their address in a directory, through directory enquiries, or on the Internet, then you can always contact the newspaper or magazine and ask the journalist who wrote the article for the contact details. If the person is famous, or a prominent businessperson, then it is highly likely they have a PR agency or agent, and the journalist can give you this information.

When telephoning, make sure you have all your information to hand and practice what you are going to say before dialling. Ask the PR agency or agent if you can write direct to that celebrity or businessperson. Often the agency will ask you to e-mail something or to write care of them. Write a letter which should be no longer than one-and-a-half sides of A4 and enclose a brief outline of your project (maximum two sides of A4) and say how you think they might be able to help you. It is not always about giving money (although that would be nice) but perhaps they'd be willing to support you in some other way, for example by visiting the school for publicity generation, donating something to be raffled or auctioned, donating equipment, helping you by putting you in touch with other potential donors.

Remember they are probably being targeted by other charities so when approaching them make sure you have all your facts to hand and know exactly what you are fundraising for and how it will make a difference (see Chapter 5.)

This area of fundraising is something that anyone can

become involved in. By enlisting people to become your eyes (readers), and giving them an indication of what to look for, you could soon have a nice pile of magazine and newspaper cuttings and a variety of people to contact. That should keep you busy for some time and could very well reap rich rewards.

In summary

- newspapers and magazines can provide a number of contacts and a wealth of information
- enlist the help of others in your school to become your readers and researchers
- carry out a survey of who reads what
- train your readers to look for relevant articles on personalities and business people who have a connection with your school or your cause, get them to cut out the articles and hand them to you
- get in touch with that person who often has a PR agency or agent working for them

8
Sources of funding – the rich and famous

So following on from the previous chapter let's examine in greater detail how to raise money from the rich and famous.

Who are they?

Well, they could include the following:
- wealthy business people/company tycoons
- celebrities i.e. pop stars, actors, sports and tv personalities, etc.
- high wealth individuals – inherited money, Lottery and Pools winners

Some of these people went to state schools. So if you haven't yet started to capture information on your pupils and their ongoing destinations then it's time you began and I mean right from infant school. These individuals could provide a rich seam of funding for the future. They have already done this as the growing list of celebrities helping schools with cash for specialist status has proved.

For example Simply Red front man Mick Hucknall gave Egerton Park School in Manchester £10,000 for its bid to become an Arts College and singer Robbie Williams wrote out a cheque for the full £50,000 for his old school, St Margaret Ward RC High School in Stoke on Trent. Businesswoman Anita Roddick, founder of the Body Shop, is a former pupil and teacher at Littlehampton Community School in West Sussex. She roped in her actor friend Woody Harrelson to help out in the school's bid to become a business and enterprise college.

It's all very well beginning the process to keep tabs on your pupils as they forge their way in the world but what about all those who couldn't wait to escape and have never been seen or heard of again, at least not within a fifty-mile radius of your playground? How do you even begin to track them down and is it worth both the time and energy?

How do you find them?

There are various ways of tracking down the rich and famous, some of which I have already mentioned for example through newspapers and magazines but there is also Debretts.

Debretts People of Today provides information on Britain's most successful people, providing biographies, areas of interest, hobbies and contact details. It is available in book, CD-ROM and online.

It includes Chairmen, Managing Directors of leading

companies, stockbrokers and bankers, editors, publishers and journalists, members of the medical profession, sportsmen and women, Church leaders, MP's, Peers and Baronets.

The CD ROM can save you both time and effort by researching key areas and people of interest. These can be tagged and then printed off. You can search on any criteria including name; education – where they went to school – it might even be your school; profession and postcode. You can target people with the same interest as you are trying to raise funds for i.e. sport, music, drama etc. and you can access full contact details including in some cases e-mail addresses.

The online version also provides weekly updates with the most current information available. An online demonstration can be provided by logging onto www.debretts.co.uk.

In addition there are mailing houses that specialise in selling mailing lists of these individuals. You can select the names you wish to purchase or rent by geographical area, targeting the people who live in your county or region. Renting usually means you have a one-off use of the list i.e. you can only mail them once, whereas purchasing the list means you can buy the names and mail them more than once. However this is often an expensive method as there is usually a minimum order value, which could prohibit anyone other than large companies, schools or consortiums of schools using this.

Internet

If you know the names of your celebrity alumni but have trouble tracking them down then not only is it worth checking out if they have their own web site but two further web sites could be of use. These are www.showcase-music.com which provides an Artists Index with contact details of their management companies or www.ukacts.com, a fairly comprehensive web site that lists actors, TV personalities and others and provides names, addresses and telephone numbers of their agents. Hollis Press and Public Relations Annual (www.hollis-pr.com) lists some PR agencies that specialise in showbusiness personalities and you can check who they represent by visiting the relevant agency web sites.

Alternatively you can try contacting the show biz reporters on the daily newspapers and asking them if they could give you contact details – they are usually very helpful.

The web site Friends Reunited is proving an interesting phenomenon. When it comes to relocating old schoolfriends, or rather trying to track them down, it could prove helpful. A recent search by a local secondary school revealed a handful of former pupils who were now working at the BBC. They may not be celebrities but they may know someone who is and be able to put you in touch with them. An introduction is extremely valuable and again provides a connection.

The school reunion

Write a letter to the editor of your local newspaper asking any old pupils to get in touch with you. Enlist the help of an ex-pupil and hold a school reunion. If school reunions are already taking place at your school then make sure you attend them, address the group, and give out any information. What is important here is that although the rich and famous may not attend the reunion someone who is still in touch with them could and could pass your message on, or put you in touch with them – again giving valuable connections.

Start cultivating the media

Keeping a high profile in your local press can also help you. Even if the wealthy individual who had once lived in your area has moved on to pastures new he may still have connections, including family, who read the local newspapers and forward articles to their famous offspring or relatives (see Chapter 13).

You could also ask your local newspaper editor if he knows of, or has written any articles on, local famous people who you may be able to approach.

Don't forget current pupils and their parents

In addition, the relatives of the celebrity, high wealth individual or business tycoon may send their children to your school. Informing and involving your parents in your fundraising is a must. If you can enthuse the parents they can enthuse others.

How do you approach them?

Write to them telling them about your fundraising

appeal and the amount you are seeking and ask for their support.

You can approach them direct if you have their address, or through their agent, PR agency or publicist.

Even if their answer to your letter is no, put them on your database and keep them informed of your fundraising progress, sending copies of press cuttings about your school and your appeal. This could be enough to make them think again about helping you in some way.

In summary

- the rich and famous can include the following:
    wealthy business people/company tycoons;
    celebrities i.e. pop stars, actors, sports and tv personalities, etc;
    high wealth individuals – inherited money, Lottery and Pools winners
- begin to capture information on your pupils and their ongoing destinations, these individuals could provide a rich seam of funding for the future
- there are various ways of tracking down the rich and famous which include:
    newspapers;
    magazines;
    Debretts People of Today;
    mailing houses;
    web sites;
    show biz reporters on the daily newspapers;
    your local newspaper editor;

Sources of funding: the rich and famous

　　Friends Reunited;
　　the school reunion.

- keeping a high profile in your local press can also help you

---

9
Sources of funding – businesses

Let's now turn to businesses as a source of potential funding.

Who are they?

Businesses can include:
- the small sole trader
- the independent local business
- a large national company
- a branch of a large national company in your location
- the head office of a large multinational or national corporation

How do you find them?

The media

Scan your local newspapers, listen to local radio, watch local television and read local business magazines. Who is advertising? Who is getting press coverage in the newspapers? What do you know about those companies? Start putting the details onto a database so that you can target them more easily.

Who do your parents work for?

Try and find out and add these companies and contacts to your database. Also look at your geographical area; what sort of things do the people spend their money on? Who would be interested in them as customers? For example, garages that sell cars are an obvious choice; solicitors who need to reach people who want to buy a house, make a will or dare I say it, get divorced are another. Local sports centres, complementary health centres and shops, the list grows.

Telephone the companies and get the name of the decision maker i.e. the director, or marketing person. If you can, speak to them direct about your appeal and try and make an appointment to see them or get them over to the school. If not, send them the details and telephone them afterwards to see if you can stimulate interest. (See Chapter 10).

Use contacts of the governing body

Use the contacts you have on the governing body to find companies and make approaches.

Local councils

Other sources of information include the web sites of your local council. Many of these have excellent resources and a searchable database of companies in your area which you can download or print off for free. If they are not available on the web site then telephone the council and ask for a list. Some councils also provide a register of businesses by industrial estate. Using council sources is quicker and easier than trawling through Yellow Pages and you are often given the name of the Managing Director or Manager, but if you haven't got it then a telephone call to obtain it is essential.

Chamber of Commerce and Institute of Directors

Every school intending to fundraise should become a member of their local Chamber of Commerce. Joining this organisation would give you an excellent opportunity to network and make direct contact with local businesses. It also helps to forge good relationships between school and business.

Some head teachers I know are also members of the Institute of Directors giving them excellent opportunities to access companies at the highest level.

Company directories

Lists can also be obtained by researching through directories at your local library. These include:

- *Kompass*
- *Key British Enterprises*

Fundraising for your school

- plus other specific trade directories

Two excellent sources, which are specially produced to aid fundraisers looking for funding opportunities, are:

UK Guide to Company Giving
Hollis Sponsorship and Donations Yearbook

The *UK Guide to Company Giving* is also available on a CD ROM. This CD ROM, developed by FunderFinder, provides details of over 500 companies giving a combined total of £290 million in cash donations to voluntary and community organisations. Search facilities help you to identify target companies by geographical area, business type, names of directors and fields of support.

The software is available in PC format only and again can be run on Windows 95 and higher. It allows you to print out the information and add your own notes.

Use your MP and local councillors

Enlist the help of your MP to introduce you to the key business people in your area. Write to him about your appeal and then call his office and invite him into the school for a meeting to explain what you are doing and why you are doing it. Ask the MP for his active support or perhaps organize an event where he will attend and invite other key business people to join you.

Also enlist the help of your local councillor. He can act as your eyes and ears on the council and put you in touch with other business people.

Do your staff know anyone working in the target companies?

Ask your staff for details of where their partners work and add them to the database. Also, before approaching a company ask staff and governors if they know anyone within that company. If they do then ask that member of staff to approach them directly (once they have been fully briefed and you have done all your homework) or use that member of staff's name to give you an introduction into the company.

Build a database

As you research the companies to target put them onto a database so that you can keep in touch with them and keep track of your approaches. It is also easier to mail merge letters to them. Categorize the companies you have researched maybe simply as A, B, C. Your A list would be top companies, large local organisations or ones that advertise locally quite heavily, and who like a high profile, these could be approached for higher sums of money. B's could be medium sized companies and good prospects for approaching and C's could perhaps be the smaller businesses that won't have a great deal to offer but could still do something to help you, perhaps by donating a raffle prize?

How do you approach them?

What is it that a school has and a business wants? If you can answer this question go to the top of the class. If you can also put a value on that commodity give yourself a gold star. But for those of you who are still struggling to answer the first question, or indeed both of the above questions, let me put you out of your misery; a school has a ready made potential audience for a company's services or products. Putting a value on accessing that audience is, however, more difficult and many schools undersell themselves. In addition, schools are often unaware of the wide range of potential areas for obtaining sponsorship from businesses.

Companies exist to sell their services or products to customers. They need to find those customers and create awareness for their products or services. This can often prove expensive and difficult. They also need to position themselves differently from their competitors. Having a clearly defined image and communicating it consistently is what gives a company a marketing edge. With the fragmentation of advertising – there are now more magazines, newspapers, television and radio channels available, not to mention the Internet – and with the rising costs of reaching that audience many businesses are turning to other more cost-effective ways of marketing. This, coupled with the growth of cause related marketing, where a company wants to associate itself with a good cause, is good news for schools.

And in case you are thinking this is just for the big boys, it isn't. Local companies need to raise brand awareness and increase brand share locally and what better way of doing this than going into partnership with a local school or group of schools?

What businesses are looking for

Companies want access to potential customers; this doesn't necessarily mean the pupils

Sources of funding: businesses

(unless the company is marketing to children) but more often means the adults in the community which the school serves. A business also wants:

- increased profile through media coverage locally, regionally, and even nationally
- the opportunity to raise its company name to a pool of future employees. This is obviously highly relevant for any secondary school. However primary schools can also use this as an incentive because for each child there is a potential adult employee
- the chance to influence their own customers in that geographical area
- the feel good factor by being involved in a good cause in the local community
- the chance for the company to look good in the eyes of its employees
- the chance to influence shareholders.

What can you offer them?

Now return to your wish list and take each item on it and write down what you can offer a company in return for their funding.

For example: Funding to buy playground equipment

You are prepared to offer a business some or all of the things listed below:

- prominent signage that promotes the company name and logo,

Fundraising for your school

> e.g. one sign facing the road where children are dropped off;
> smaller signs around the playground

- an acknowledgment sign in the reception area and/or hall
- the chance for the company director to officially open the new playground or present the equipment with a photographer present and the opportunity for publicity around this. You could also invite some parents/governors to attend the opening.
- a mention in the school prospectus
- the equipment painted in the company's corporate colours.

Another example: Funding for your school newsletter

You are prepared to offer:

- the company name and logo on the front cover
- the opportunity for the company to place an advertisement, and/or to provide a regular column
- an acknowledgement in the reception area or hall with the company name on your plaque of patrons or supporters
- a link from the school web site to the company web site and vice versa
- the opportunity for the company to use the school as an example/case study in the company's corporate literature.

Do you get the idea?

List the benefits to a company for being involved with your school

Here you need to address the questions 'Why should we?' 'What's in it for us?' 'How will my company benefit?'

If one of the benefits is access to a potential audience then specify how many and what kind of audience? For example, let's say you have 500 pupils. For this exercise let's assume each pupil has two parents or guardians, that immediately gives the company access to a potential audience of 1,000 (1500 if you include the pupils, depending on their age). Now add to this the number of staff, governors, and their partners and that could make 2,100. Let's also assume that each child has two grandparents, that gives us an audience of 2,200 and if we include aunts and uncles, and possibly other community users of our school, we can further increase the number of potential customers who will see the company name on the newsletter or school prospectus. If you have offered the company a prominent sign visible to passing traffic then you could also include the approximate number of cars driving along that busy road.

As to the type of audience, this depends on the area surrounding your school i.e. your catchment area. Do the local people live in terraced housing, council housing and have lower incomes, or are you situated in an area where residents are mainly professional and better off and live in semi-detached or detached housing? What is the socio-economic profile of your target audience? Scottish Power became involved in one secondary school in Hampshire because it is based in a large council estate and the company wanted to target this kind of household.

In return for their investment in your school the company will not only have access to a target audience but it will also have the opportunity to sell to that audience and promote itself in the right light. It will enjoy increased name awareness and an increased profile.

Define the deal

This is often the tricky bit. How much is the sponsorship deal worth? What are you going to ask for? Start by looking at how much it will cost you to buy that playground equipment, produce the school newsletter, buy books for the library, or take the children on that outing. Now go back to your package of what you are offering and the benefits to the company – how much is that worth to the company? If they were to get the same exposure, say through local advertising or a flyer, how much would it cost them? Some basic research will answer this question for you – simply telephone your local newspaper and ask them for their advertising rates. Advertising is expensive and is not targeted whereas what you are offering is a carefully targeted opportunity over a period. In marketing principles people buy what they are familiar with and exposure over a period is far more successful than a one off advertisement.

In my experience many schools undervalue what they have to offer. I often tell them to treble the figure they first thought of and sometimes even quadruple it.

If for example you were encouraging a local motor dealer to sponsor you, or give you funding in return for promoting them for a year within your school and on school material etc, they would only need to sell one car to your audience to reap their reward; in fact they would probably make considerable money on the sponsorship deal unless your school happens to be an area of low car ownership. Some research beforehand should flag this up for you.

Do you offer sole sponsorship?

Going for one sponsor will save you time and energy and companies are usually more interested in sole sponsorship. If this fails, you can start to look for a number of sponsors per area, or break your proposal down so that each individual company sponsors a different element of the proposal.

> **Remember you are not begging. You are offering a strong proposition to a company.**

You have something they want. You can help them market their organization more efficiently and more cost effectively. The company builds stronger links with their community and the children, and the school builds stronger links with business community. Surely that has got to be worth something!

The letter to businesses

Here you need to write a persuasive letter, one that is hard for the businessperson to ignore, a letter that has something in it for them.

So how do you do this?

Ensure that your letter is personalized i.e. it is addressed to a named person and not 'Dear Sir/Madam'. Then follow the basic principles of copywriting which is summed up by the acronym AIDA.

> Attention, Interest, Desire, Action

Before we look at how to do this in detail it might be helpful for you to understand how the letter is read. Research has shown there is a sequence to this. The eyes flick through the following:

1. The senders address – who is it from?
2. The greeting – If it is personalized it is more likely to be read
3. The first sentence – What is this letter all about and why should I read it?
4. Skim to the last part
5. If you are lucky, your letter is well written with lots of benefits to the reader, then they will go back to the first sentence and read it through properly, increasing your chances of getting a response.

So the first sentence is the key to holding and arousing the readers' interest.

Get attention

You have only a couple of seconds to do this before they bin your letter so you need to put your key benefit first. Tell the reader why you are writing to him in particular and why he should read the letter; what he might lose if he ignores the message. You can start your letter with a question or bold statement.

For example:

How would you like to reach over 1,000 carefully targeted customers direct?

How would you like to raise your company profile in the Anytown area?

Build interest

From your opening you need to go straight into your body copy and make sure you have strong benefits that will leap out at the reader. Avoid waffle.

For example following on from our Attention question your body copy would read something like this:

How would you like to reach over 1,000 carefully targeted customers direct?

Well now you can. By sponsoring our new playground equipment your company could promote its name and services direct to over 1,000 carefully targeted prospective customers. What's more, because our school is situated on Anytown High Street, your company name would be visible to all the vehicles and pedestrians passing by, therefore considerably increasing your name exposure on a regular basis.

Then go on to develop the interest with a second and further benefits. You must get the reader saying, 'Yes, I must have some of that!'

For example:

In addition, we will acknowledge your sponsorship in our school prospectus which is circulated to nearly 2,000 people and in our regular Newsletter produced each term (4 times a year) thus promoting your company on a regular basis.

Stimulate desire

Bring in other benefits. Explain how the reader may lose out unless he takes action.

For example:

In return for your sponsorship your company will not only have access to a target audience but it will also have the opportunity to sell to that audience and promote itself. It will enjoy increased name awareness and an enhanced profile.

Our sponsorship package starts at £500 for sponsoring one piece of playground equipment and rises to £5,000 for exclusive sponsorship. For exclusive sponsorship I can offer your company not only the options above but also a number of additional opportunities. These can include:

- *prominent signage around the playground that promotes your company name and logo*
- *an acknowledgment sign in our reception area highly visible to all visitors*
- *the chance for a company director to officially open the new playground or present the equipment with the opportunity for publicity around this.*
- *the equipment painted in the company's corporate colours.*

- *acknowledgement on our web site with a link to your company web site, thus increasing traffic to your own web site.*

Get action

Then go on to ask them to take action.

For example:

I enclose details of the sponsorship opportunities available and would be very happy to discuss this with you. The package can be tailored to suit. These sponsorship opportunities could provide your company with a highly cost-effective form of advertising and marketing and at the same time with the satisfaction of knowing that it is helping local children in a local school. Please tick the fax back enclosed to indicate your interest or call me on 10234 56789.

Then personally sign it.

When writing this type of letter a common mistake is to put too much waffle at the beginning about your school. The reader doesn't need all that. They want to know what's in it for them! Don't be shy about what you are offering; a good offer must be impossible to ignore but don't make it hard for the person to respond, give them a fax back, and/or e-mail response and let them tick boxes.

Position the letter well on the page and use block paragraphs with double spacing between each paragraph. Make sure you allow enough space for a signature, job title and name and staple pages together if more than one. You can use capitals, italics or underlining but do not clutter unnecessarily.

Phase the letters out

Rather than sending say 1,000 in one hit, send a few each week, or every two weeks, whatever is manageable for you. Then, with a copy of the letter in front of you, telephone them to follow up. (See Chapter 10).

Example letter

J. Brown
Managing Director
ACME Limited
Any Street
Anytown
PO11 0PL

Date

Dear Mr. Brown

How would you like to reach over 1,000 carefully targeted customers direct?
Well now you can. By sponsoring our new playground equipment your company could promote its name and services direct to over 1,000 carefully targeted prospective customers. What's more, because our school is situated on Anytown High Street, your company name would be visible to all the vehicles and pedestrians passing by therefore considerably increasing your name exposure on a regular basis.

In addition, we will acknowledge your sponsorship in our school prospectus which is circulated to nearly 2,000 people and in our regular Newsletter produced each term (4 times a year) thus promoting your company on a regular basis.

In return for your sponsorship your company will not only have access to a target audience but it will also have the opportunity to sell to that audience and promote itself. It will enjoy increased name awareness and an enhanced profile.

Our sponsorship package starts at £500 for sponsoring one piece of playground equipment and rises to £5,000 for exclusive sponsorship. For exclusive sponsorship I can offer your company not only the options above but a number of additional opportunities. These can include:

- prominent signage around the playground that promotes your company name and logo
- an acknowledgment sign in our reception area highly visible to all visitors
- the chance for a company director to officially open the new playground or present the equipment with the opportunity for publicity around this
- the equipment painted in the company's corporate colours
- acknowledgment on our web site with a link to your company web site, thus increasing traffic to your own web site.

And of course you can promote your involvement with our school in your own company publicity and marketing material.

I enclose details of the sponsorship opportunities available and would be very happy to discuss this with you. The package can be tailored to suit. These sponsorship opportunities could provide your company with a highly cost-effective form of advertising and marketing and at the same time with the satisfaction of knowing that it is helping local children in a local school. Please tick the fax back enclosed to indicate your interest or call me direct on 10234 56789.

Yours sincerely,

B. Smith
Head Teacher

Be positive and confident about what you are offering. There are some great opportunities for local businesses to be gained from being involved in schools: they just need it pointed out to them.

In summary

- research companies to target from:
    newspapers and magazines;
    local council web sites;
    directories in local libraries;
    UK Guide to Company Giving;
    Hollis Sponsorship and Donations;
    Chamber of Commerce;
    Institute of Directors;
    Your MP and local councillors;
- build a database to help you keep track of your approaches
- categorize these companies by the level of their possible donation
- define what you can offer a company in return for sponsorship or a donation
- list the benefits to that company for sponsoring you
- work out how much that sponsorship is worth to the potential funder
- ensure that your letter is personalized in that it is addressed to a named contact
- the first sentence is key to arousing and holding their interest
- build their interest by making sure there are benefits to the company for becoming involved with your school
- phase the letters out and follow them up with a telephone call.

10
Approaching sponsors by telephone

I mentioned very briefly in the previous chapter about telephoning businesses to follow up your letter. You can of course call them before you send a letter to see if you can stimulate some interest from them. Whichever you choose cold calling people you don't know to try and sell them something is guaranteed to strike fear into anyone's heart. The head teachers and teachers I've met would rather deal with half a dozen rampaging pupils before first break than pick up the dreaded instrument and speak to a business person to persuade them to part with their hard-earned cash – and who can blame them? Telemarketing, as it is officially called, is not for the faint hearted. Neither is it for the inexperienced. It is a skill and, like any other skill, it can be learnt.

Preparation is the key to success and before you even pick up the telephone you will need to be clear about the following:

1 What area do you require funding for? Be clear about your funding requirement. Focus on one area only at a time.

2   What are you offering the company in return for its support? Put together a package that also demonstrates the benefits to that company for supporting you.

3   Put a value on that and have all this information ready to hand before you make your call.

4   Be clear about the benefits to a company in return for supporting you

5   Research the companies to target, prioritize these and draw up a list.

6   Set yourself targets – how many calls are you going to make per day, per week etc? Make sure it is realistic.

So you lift the telephone and make your call and it is now that you may encounter the person who thinks they are being paid to keep you out.

Getting past the telephonist

Make up your mind what you want from the call and stick to it. In the first instance your objective will be to get past the telephonist. Tell yourself this is your call, you are in control. Don't allow anyone else to hijack it. You need to sound confident and convincing. Believe in what you are offering. You have an excellent opportunity for a business to raise its profile and possibly win more customers. If you say this to yourself you will evoke positive messages to the brain, which will in turn affect your body language and make you feel and sound more confident. If you hesitate, mumble or start dithering then the telephonist will use it as an opportunity to take control, with the result that they will not put you through, and they may even take it upon themselves to make a decision on behalf of the boss, which could be the wrong decision and a missed opportunity for both your school and that company.

When speaking to the telephonist keep your talking to a minimum, don't go into the details of what you are offering to this person because you are selling to the wrong person who will invariably misinterpret it, not understand what you are trying to say, or make the decision to say no themselves. You need to put pressure on the telephonist to put you through to the right person, who you will have determined beforehand by making a general enquiry call.

When speaking to the telephonist the name of the person you wish to speak to and your name are the only information they require. Don't answer their questions, which is a natural response, but reply with a question instead. For example if they say 'What's it about?' you answer, 'Is he in?' This takes a bit of practice but is highly effective.

In order to aid authority try using your full name and your position, for example Mrs Smith rather than your first name only. Use your title especially if you are head teacher.

> The way you sound is more important that what you are saying.

Remember they can't see you – they only have your tone of voice to respond to and if you sound important the telephonist will think you are important and respond accordingly. Try raising your voice; sound crisp, efficient, businesslike.

If you are having difficulty with a particular telephonist who stubbornly refuses to put you through then try calling at a different time of the day, say the lunch period when the relief telephonist may be on duty and may not be so efficient as the full-time one. Try calling later in the day, after hours for example, when the system is switched over to night service and you may find yourself sailing through, or even talking directly to the person you require. This is obviously dependent on the industry sector you are targeting.

Use powerful words, for example, 'I really do **need** to speak to him'. **Need** implies urgency.

So having got through what happens next? Now to the sales pitch.

Set your objective

You need to be clear what you want to achieve from the call because this will drive it. Here are some objectives for your call:

- to secure an appointment with the prospective sponsor
- to arrange a time for them to visit your school
- to find out the name of the decision maker and other relevant information.

Failing all that, to send some literature about your sponsorship or funding opportunity and agree a call back time to discuss.

The stages of a call

There are, broadly speaking, three stages in the call structure.

Stage 1: opening the call

Make your introduction as succinct as possible. You should say your name, position and the name of your school clearly and slowly. Your call will be interrupting the other person and it will take them a while to switch from what they were doing to listening to you.

Your voice must convey a great deal. Don't shout and don't talk too quietly. Look and be alert. If your body is slouched your voice will sound slouched. Use the same body language on the telephone as you would normally face-to-face.

After your introduction use an 'open' question. I am sure you all know that 'open' questions begin with:

Who

What

Where

When

How

Why.

These are the key to effective interviewing and telephoning as they will get the prospective sponsor to open up and start a conversation with you, which is what you are aiming for.

As the beginning of the call is the most nerve-racking part of it I recommend that you write out your introduction and your first 'open' question.

For example:

'Hello, Mr Brown, I'm Margaret Smith, head teacher of Anytown Junior School. We've put together a sponsorship offer for businesses, which might interest you as it guarantees you reaching a target audience of at least 2,000 potential customers in your area. We're seeking businesses that would be interested in sponsoring our newsletter and in return can offer a number of advertising and editorial opportunities. How does this sound to you?' Or 'How do you currently market your services to your prospective customers?'

From the introduction above I have led directly into an 'open' question to get Mr Brown talking. If you ask a 'closed' question, for example ' Would you be interested?' or 'Is this something you would be interested in?' you are giving Mr Brown the opportunity of saying 'No' to you right from the beginning. If you do find yourself asking this closed question and Mr Brown says 'No, not interested' ask him an open question, for example 'Why is that?' That way you can draw more information from him, and if you've got your list of what you are offering and the benefits of your sponsorship offer in front of you, or firmly in your mind, you may be able to persuade him otherwise.

Here is another example:

'Hello Mr Jones, I'm Bob White, head teacher of ABC Secondary School. We're applying to become a specialist sports college and we're looking for local businesses who would like to become partners in our bid, guaranteeing that business not only access to a wide target audience but also the chance to promote itself to our students, a pool of potential employees.

How interested would your company be in this?'

If Mr Jones says, 'Not very interested', you can respond by asking '**Why** is this?' Again asking an 'open' question in a pleasant, curious manner.

Stage 2: asking questions and presenting benefits

You may need to follow up the response from your opening (Stage 1). with further open questions, so be prepared for this. Unless you are very lucky and Mr Brown says that he is interested in what you might be offering, in which case you can skip Stage 2 and go straight to Stage 3 and arrange an appointment.

Here are some examples of open situation questions, which can be used in Stage 2.

- how do you currently market/advertise your services/products?
- how do you currently recruit employees?
- how important is it for your company to have good community relations?

And you also need to start selling in the benefits of what you are offering, although not too many – remember your objective is to get a meeting or get them to visit your school; just one or two to whet their appetite.

From the answers given to the **open situation questions** you are determining a need or possible problem that you could help solve by one or some of the benefits you are offering.

For example:

You: 'How do you currently market your services Mr Jones?' **(Open situation question)**

Mr Jones: 'Mainly through the local newspaper.'

You: 'What sort of response does that give you?' **(Open situation question)**

Mr Jones: 'It's OK. Could be better.' **(Possible need here to get better response to current advertising)**

You: 'Advertising in the newspaper is expensive, isn't it, and of course it doesn't always go right to the people you want to see it. With our newsletter it goes direct to 2,000 adults who live on your doorstep and of course it's cheaper than advertising in the local newspaper and would help build a good profile for your company.' **(Here I have sold in the benefits of sponsoring our school newsletter) i.e.**

- it is cheaper than advertising in the local newspaper;
- it will go straight to their target customers;
- it will raise the company's profile.

Have some pertinent questions mapped out beforehand. Alternatively you may have identified this company as a potential sponsor from its advertisements in the newspaper, both the vacancies section or general advertising and can refer to this in your call. For example 'I see you advertise regularly in the local newspaper, Mr Jones. What kind of response do you get?'

What often prevents people from being successful is that they are afraid to ask open questions or they have lost the habit of doing so.

Buying signals

Throughout the call you must listen actively for buying signals. These can come through at any time and can simply be people saying things like, 'Really!' or 'That's interesting.' You should be prepared to pick up on these and reinforce the benefit that has prompted them to say this, then go on to ask for the appointment.

For example if the prospective sponsor asks

'How much does it cost?' this is a buying signal. He wouldn't be asking if he wasn't vaguely interested. This is where you can say 'We have a number of sponsorship opportunities', then you go on to close the call by saying something along the lines of:

'Why don't I come out and see you and then we can run through this in greater detail and you can see if it might be appropriate to you, and if you'd like to get involved. Or you can visit the school: which would you prefer?'

Stage 3: closing the call

As in the previous example always give them an alternative – it helps them to make a decision. For example: 'Why don't you come out to the school and then you can see for yourself what we do and how we might work together for our mutual benefit; when would be convenient for you **next week or the week after?**'

Once having made the appointment, confirm it and close the call, don't be tempted to talk on or you could find yourself overselling.

Remember throughout the call that it is **your** call –

you are in charge of it – you are driving it. Do not fall into the trap, as people so often do, of waiting for the prospective sponsor either to ask a question, ask for details, or ask for someone to come out and see them. They probably won't and you may simply get the fob off 'Just put some details in the post.'

If this happens by all means do so but follow it up with a telephone call afterwards. Your response might be something like this:

'I'd be happy to put details in the post to you, Mr Jones. I'll give you a chance to look through it, when would be the best time to call you back?'

Keep a list of the open questions in front of you: Who, What, Where, When, How and Why.

And don't give up

Persistence pays off. Be positive. If you have put together a good package be confident in what you are offering businesses.

In summary

- do your preparation before you make the call, know what you are offering and the benefits to that company
- make up your mind what you want from the call and stick to it
- set your objectives beforehand – ultimately try and get an appointment or get them to visit the school
- when speaking to the telephonist try and keep

your talking to a minimum, you need to speak to the decision maker
- there are three stages to the call:
the opening;
asking questions and presenting benefits;
closing the call and getting the visit
- use 'open' questions to get a conversation going
- listen for buying signals when they show interest and capitalize on these by suggesting an appointment or visit
- be confident, positive, polite and persistent

11
The face to face meeting

After all that hard work of preparing the appeal and telephoning endlessly trying to drum up support, someone agrees to see you. They indicate they are mildly interested in listening to what you have to say and once you've got over the initial shock and euphoria the doubts begin to set in – how are you going to handle this meeting? You don't want to blow it. You might only have this one chance to make a good enough impression to secure some vital funding so you need to make it your best shot.

In order to be successful you need to be prepared for the meeting, know how to control and steer the conversation, how to present the benefits of giving to your good cause and how to ask for the support or cash. A tall order, but possible. If you've got as far as a meeting then take heart – you're a short step away from getting a commitment. Whether the meeting is taking place on their premises or yours the basic principles are the same.

Who should go?

To answer this question you need to ask whom the meeting is with? If it is with the Chief Executive or Managing Director of a sizeable company then preferably it should be the head teacher, or someone of equivalent rank. If the company is smaller, or the position of the person you are seeing less senior, then perhaps someone other than the Head can attend. But whoever goes it's not so much a question of seniority as knowledge. It's no good sending someone, whoever they are, if they have little knowledge or enthusiasm about your project, or if they are pretty poor at communication. The best person to attend any face to face meeting is the one who knows all about the project, and who is passionate about it. Knowledge and enthusiasm will come across and are far more important than 'rank'.

Set your objectives

What do you want to achieve from this meeting? Will you be able to get a commitment from the person you are seeing there and then or will he have to refer to someone else? Will it take a couple of meetings before you get a decision? If possible aim high, try to get some kind of firm commitment before you leave, a pledge of money or equipment would be nice, but it may not be possible. If not then make sure you leave the dialogue open, you may need to go back to see them again, or invite them into your school, or you may need to send further information. Whichever, try to ensure you get a timetable or date before the end of your meeting.

> To fail to prepare is to prepare to fail

What do you know about the prospective sponsor? What do you know about their company? Have you read anything about them in your local press? Is the school already involved with the company and if so, how?

Are you clear about your own project and what you are asking for? Have you done all your homework?

Check you have all the right material at your fingertips

Do you have a leaflet that you can leave with them? Do you have all the details and information to hand? Scrabbling around for it makes you look unprepared and unprofessional. Will they want to be involved with a school that gives out this kind of impression? I doubt it particularly if you are asking them to part with their money.

Which brings us onto another vital point and one that has been mentioned before in previous chapters: know what you are offering in return for support, be clear about your funding requirements, have your package ready and know the benefits that the company or individual could enjoy by being involved with your school.

If you are visiting their premises arrive a few minutes early (never late) and sit in reception, take a look around; you can learn an awful lot there that might help you. For example there may be a press cuttings file in reception which could give you valuable background information on the company and what is important to them in terms of their media profile. Or there may be a company or staff newsletter on display and awards on the wall.

> You never get a second chance to make a first impression.

If the prospective sponsor is visiting your school, ensure they are met and dealt with promptly and in a friendly welcoming manner. First impressions count and this goes for personal appearance too, so be smart, well groomed and professional looking. Smile, give good eye contact and a firm dry handshake.

Before we look at how to **open the conversation** it may be helpful here for you to understand **buying motivations.**

Buying motivations

When you first meet that prospective sponsor he will probably be wary, sceptical and hesitant. These are the **negative buying motivations**. If you don't gain that person's confidence at the beginning of the conversation then you never will and you won't get the support you are seeking.

The negative buying motivations can be summed up as follows:

- I don't trust you.
- I don't need you.
- No, I don't think you can help me.

- I'm in no hurry – I'll think about it and get back to you.
- No, I don't think we're interested.

So in order to win support you need to switch your potential sponsor over to the **positive buying motivations.** These are:

- I am important.
- Consider my needs.
- Will your ideas help me?
- What are the details?
- What are the problems?
- I approve.

Switching from negative to positive

So how do you switch your prospective sponsor from the negative buying motivations to the positive buying motivations?

The first two stages in the positive buying motivation process are crucial:

- I am important.
- Consider my needs.

Opening the conversation

Once in front of someone, the urge is to leap right into giving the details of your project, how wonderful your school is and how much money you need to raise; don't. You need to win them over first and in order to do this you need to make them feel valued and important. The way to do this is by getting them to talk and there are two things that people like talking about: themselves and their companies. So you need to ask good **open questions,** for example:

- What do they do?
- How does their business operate?
- What are the challenges they face?
- How many people do they employ?
- How long have they been in business?
- Who are their customers?

In your conversation you can refer to the research you've already carried out which demonstrates that you are genuinely interested in them.

Don't hand any of your literature to a prospect at the beginning of the meeting. This will guarantee that he will be looking at it and not listening to you, or wanting to participate in the discussion. Save your literature until the end of the meeting.

Some other ways of making the individual feel important are:

- use the person's name in your conversation, particularly at the beginning of the meeting.
- listen to them – and I mean really listen. Listening is the highest form of courtesy.

Having switched the prospect over to the first two positive buying motivations, you will then need to take the others into consideration. These are:

- Will your ideas help me?

- What are the details?
- What are the problems?
- I approve.

Selling in benefits

Sponsorship is a two-way street: they want something from you and you want something from them. From your conversation you will be able to pick up clues as to what they are interested in and match this with the benefits you have to offer and which will excite them. You need to present your project to them i.e. tell them about it and importantly tell them how you think it **will help them.**

Once the potential sponsor starts asking you questions, you have interest. This means you have reached the **'what are the details?'** stage of the buying motivations. Answer them honestly and clearly and if you don't understand the question, or are not sure how to answer it, then ask them to clarify what they mean.

When and if the potential sponsor starts putting up reasons not to become involved, or donate to your school, you have reached the **'what are the problems stage?'** Don't dismay: if you overcome this you are only a short step away from getting a commitment. It may be that the potential sponsor says that he'd like to help but hasn't got any money in his budget at the moment. Ask him when his budgeting process starts and his new financial year begins because you could offer to start the sponsorship now but get a written commitment that the money can come out of next year's budget? Or perhaps you could stage the sponsorship or donation to make it easier for him to give. If the potential sponsor says that he is really interested but needs to talk to his fellow directors then fine, ask when he will do this and when you can get back in contact.

Getting a commitment

Once you have overcome any problems you can go on to ask for a commitment and don't be afraid to do this; many people are because they are afraid of being rejected. Simply ask if they are interested in helping your school and if so how? If they say 'no' then ask them 'why?' The reason they give you could very well be overcome, or they may be labouring under a misapprehension about what sponsorship involves.

If you are fortunate enough to get a commitment then thank them, say what will happen next, change the subject and leave. Don't be tempted to talk on about the project or your school, a common error and one that could cost you dearly as you could find yourself 'overselling' and saying something that will make them change their mind. Leave literature if you have it, but essentially shut up and get out.

In summary

- be prepared for the meeting, know how to steer the conversation, how to present the benefits of giving to your cause and how to ask for support or cash
- the best person to attend the meeting is the one

The face to face meeting

who knows about the project, is enthusiastic and passionate about it

- if you don't get a commitment at the first meeting but they show interest get a date when you can go back to them
- research the company you are visiting, find out all you can about them
- check you have the right material with you
- if you are visiting their premises arrive early and take a look around reception while you wait, it could provide you with valuable information about that company
- if the prospective sponsor is visiting your school make sure he is met and dealt with promptly in a warm and friendly manner
- in order to win support you need to take a sincere interest in the prospective sponsor so get them to talk about their business
- don't hand out any literature at the beginning of your meeting, or they will be reading it and not listening to you

12
Giving a presentation

In the previous chapter we looked at presenting your project on a one to one basis but what if you have to present it to a group of people, perhaps the Chamber of Commerce, or Rotary or a community group? How do you handle this? Firstly don't worry if you are nervous; nearly everyone is when they need to make a speech. This is often because everyone will be looking at you. But instead of thinking about all those people looking at you reverse it – you need to think of yourself as giving out. You must tell yourself that you are in control. Why? Because the brain is the most powerful organ in your body and you need to train it to respond in the right way.

For example if you are saying to yourself, 'This is going to be awful. I'm dreading this. They'll ask me questions I can't answer. I just know I'll stammer. I wish this was over', then this will send negative messages to your body language, which in turn will be defensive; you will stammer and be ineffectual. So you need to correct this inner negative voice and convert it to a positive one. Here's how.

Overcoming nerves

1 Tell yourself that the audience wants you to be good. They are not trying to trip you up or trap you. They are genuinely interested in hearing what you have to say otherwise why would they be there?

2 Tell yourself that you have a good cause and that you also have many opportunities that could help these businesses.

3 Tell yourself this is not a life and death situation.

Human memory for the spoken word is extremely short, so even if you make a hash of things people will have often forgotten your speech within hours. This is why you should ask the organizer for a list of delegates so that you can write to each individual afterwards to remind them of your talk and your fundraising appeal and request an interview to discuss the opportunities for them to become involved. It's also why you need to have some literature with you to hand out.

Before your talk, rehearse it in front of one or two helpful colleagues. You don't have to memorize it as this can make you even more nervous. It is not a memory test. However, memorizing the beginning can often help people (it does me). This is when you are at your most nervous and once over this hurdle your overhead or PowerPoint slides can help you to remember key stages of your talk as can small index cards with headings and one or two salient points on them.

Here are some others ways to help you overcome nervousness especially right at the beginning of your talk when the trick is to divert eyes from you.

Stand a chart some way from you, or put up a visual and ask people to look at it. That way you can chat quite happily about what is on the chart without people looking at you.

For example, you may want to have a visual of your fundraising target, or your school, how it looks now and how you would like it to look with help from the audience. Or you could use a video of the pupils performing an activity, or undertaking a project that would be expanded if your fundraising targets can be met. Think creatively around an opening.

Another way of diverting the focus from you is to start with a question to the audience, for example, 'How many of you here today think your school days were the best of years of your life?' (Hands up). Then ask, 'The gentleman in the red tie, why do you think that?' All eyes are now on him. You can now pick up on what he said by going straight into your talk, for example 'Our aim is to make our pupils school days the best days of their lives and we can only do that by developing and enhancing the facilities we have ...'

It is a good way of getting audience participation and any talk that can involve people will help them remember it afterwards.

Preparing your presentation

Who are your audience? Are they large business concerns or small businesses? Can the organizers give you this information? Ask them and then see if you need to adapt the content of your presentation accordingly. For example, you don't want to be asking them for thousands of pounds when they can only give you hundreds: you will put them off. You may, of course, be giving your talk to a community group, again what type of community, what do you think their concerns or interests will be? Try and be imaginative and address their needs, show them how becoming involved can help them; think of the benefits to them, rather than to you.

Look at time constraints. Don't be too ambitious by trying to cram everything into your talk. Be selective with your content you don't have to go into the history of the school, or details of the last OFSTED, rather give them information about your project or appeal, why you need this money, how much you need, how it will make a difference to the community and pupils, how they can become involved, the benefits to them and what to do next.

Watch your body language

You have 90 seconds to make an impression that will last throughout the presentation so make sure it is the right impression. Convey friendliness by using open gestures showing the palms of your hands.

Always stand rather than sit. It aids authority. Your energy level is different when you stand and you look more powerful. Do not be tempted into giving your talk to the only friendly face and ignoring the rest, let your eyes sweep the room.

Some openings

The most important parts of any presentation is the beginning and the end, when the audience's attention is at its peak. Make these as memorable as possible but don't attempt humour if you are not an accomplished speaker, as it can backfire. Here is one way you can start your presentation:

- welcome them
- introduce yourself
- tell them what your intention is e.g. 'Over the next twenty minutes I will tell you about our ambitious plans to raise funds for our school.'
- the Route Map – e.g. 'I will explain why we need these extra funds, how it will help benefit the pupils and the community, what businesses can gain by becoming involved and how they can become involved.'
- the Rules of the Road – e.g. 'I will be happy to take questions at the end.'

Then go into your presentation using possibly one of the techniques detailed previously.

The ending

The last thing the audience sees is the freshest that they take away with them so your finish is crucial. You could, perhaps, prepare a special visual aid summarizing your presentation. In all events the ending should include:

- a summary of the salient facts

- a recommendation of a course of action – support us now!
- a proposal for the next step – contact me to discuss how we can tailor an opportunity to suit your company
- a description of the supporting literature which you are distributing
- thanks for patient attention
- invitation to ask questions.

A word about questions

Taking questions is another worrying aspect of public speaking. If the thought of this terrifies you then when you give your 'Rules of the Road' say that you will answer questions individually after the presentation.

It will be necessary to give presentations to a variety of groups if you wish to fundraise. For each group ask yourself what they want from you, and tailor your approach accordingly; don't come up with one 'fit all' speech, but adapt to your audience and be aware of time constraints. When you rehearse your speech it will be shorter than when you stand up to talk as you will add in other points and fill it out with er's and ums. So allowing for this, your rehearsed talk should be at least ten minutes shorter than the actual one.

And finally, believe in yourself and your cause. Remember, if you have passion it will show through and win hearts, hopefully pockets too.

In summary

- think of yourself as giving out – the audience are genuinely interested in hearing what you have to say
- tell yourself you have a good cause and there are good opportunities for businesses to become involved with your school
- believe in what you are saying, be passionate about it, it will show through
- ask the organizers for a list of delegates so that you can write to them afterwards
- have some literature with you to hand out
- adapt your presentation according to your audience, and ask yourself what they want from you
- look at time constraints, don't be too ambitious with content

13
Building a media profile

The media is a very powerful tool and one that schools are often afraid of harnessing. Why? Because most schools' experience of the media is negative. But not all media coverage is bad and when it comes to fundraising the media can prove a very valuable ally in helping you communicate to your local community your fundraising objectives. A media profile can also stimulate donations, offers of help from the community, and generate interest from local companies.

So how do you get a good media profile? How do you target the journalist? What kind of fundraising stories can you generate and how can you increase your chances of getting media coverage?

The days when reporters were truly roving looking for good stories have long gone. We are all under pressure to produce more to tighter deadlines on fewer resources and journalists are no different. By giving them news stories you are helping them to do their job and getting your vital fundraising appeal in the media. In order to do this you need to give the journalist your news in the format and language they like – you need to write them a 'news release'. You also need to ensure that you give them the right kind of story.

What is newsworthy?

There are many stories to tell and listed below are just a few examples. Your first big story is the launch of your fundraising appeal. You've done all the legwork, you have an appeal name and a logo and you want to tell your local community how much you need to raise and why you need to raise it.

You will then need to follow this up with other stories and drip feed these to the media to ensure you keep your appeal in the public eye. These news stories can include for example:

- receiving your first donation
- milestones in your fund raising appeal e.g. the first £1,000, the first year
- news about forthcoming fundraising events in school and outside – like organizing a sponsored bad hair day for pupils, or a non-uniform day to raise money, a disco, dance etc.
- follow-up stories on how much you raised through your bad hair day event etc
- joint stories with donors i.e. companies who give you money or help – they usually love the additional media coverage and this, after all, is a big incentive for them to give to you

- pleas for more funds
- fundraising events around special days e.g. Valentine's Day, Mother's Day, school anniversaries

These are just a few ideas and there are many more once you start thinking 'media'. When your fundraising committee meet they should always discuss what stories they can feed to the local media so ensure this is an agenda item.

Who will be interested in my news story?

The target media will vary from area to area but can include:

- local daily newspapers
- weekly newspapers
- weekly or monthly freesheets
- local radio
- regional radio
- local television
- regional television
- specialist local educational media
- community newspapers and freesheets

You will need to get contact names. This could be the education or community journalist, the women's editor, or simply the news desk or editor. Telephone to get details then add this to a database. This will help you when sending out your news release and as journalists frequently change jobs will assist you in keeping track of them.

How to get onto television and radio

Getting onto television and radio is more difficult than getting into print simply because television and radio do not have the same amount of 'space' dedicated to news stories. Research your local radio or television station, and the most suitable programmes for your news story, and submit your news release to the producer of that programme, or to a correspondent or reporter. However radio and television get many of their news stories from the press. So even though you may not have targeted radio or television with your news story you could still find yourself being interviewed because they have picked up your story from the local newspaper. Many local and regional radio stations have web sites with contact names, and e-mail addresses, and you can send your news release direct to the producer or presenter.

Writing the news release

There is a style and structure to the news release and by following it you will increase your chances of gaining media coverage.

When constructing a news release you need to think of a triangle or pyramid.

The whole story including the angle is contained in the first paragraph and then the story is fleshed out in subsequent paragraphs. If you study newspapers you will see this style in evidence.

Constructing the news release

Headline – an idea of what the story is about

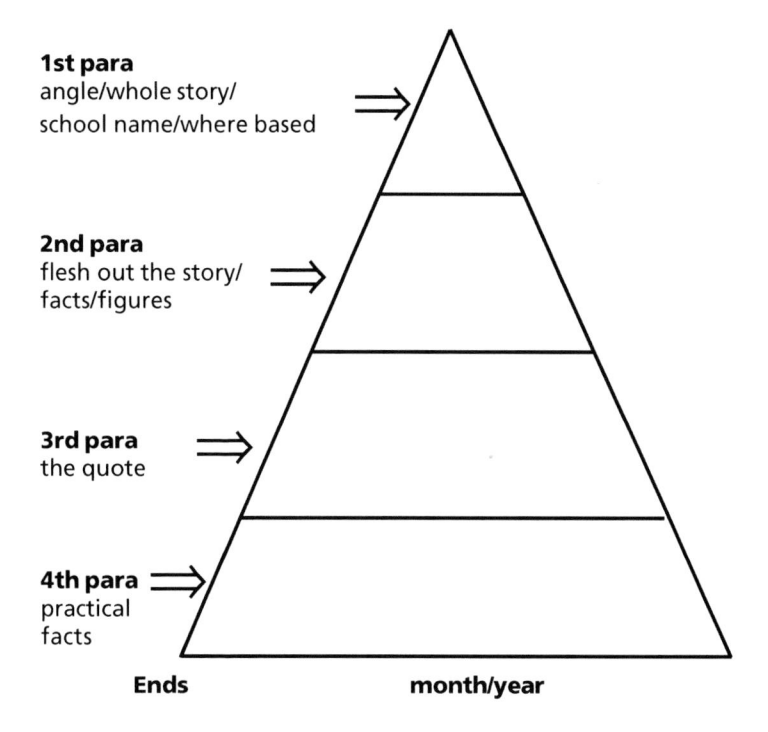

1st para
angle/whole story/
school name/where based

2nd para
flesh out the story/
facts/figures

3rd para
the quote

4th para
practical facts

Ends   **month/year**

For further information contact:
Contact Name, School Name, Location,
Telephone, e-mail address.

Fundraising for your school

Writing the news release – step by step

Let's take the launch of our fundraising appeal and draft a news release around it.

The headline

This must encapsulate the story. The headline is there to catch the journalist's eye and tell him what the story is about. Your headline will rarely if ever be used by the newspaper or magazine. The journalist, editor, or sub-editor will put their own title to the story, which best fits the style of their publication.

Example headline:

Anytown Primary School Launches Fundraising Appeal for New Swimming Pool

This tells the journalist exactly what the story is about. You don't have to be a Sun sub-editor and come up with catchy headlines.

The first paragraph

This is the key to the release. It must contain the whole story, the angle and your school's name and where based. Can you tell your whole story in one short paragraph?

Here is an example of a first paragraph following on from our headline.

Example – First paragraph

Anytown Primary School, based in Treetown, is launching a £250,000 fundraising appeal, 'Swimalong', to build a new swimming pool in the school grounds, which will benefit both the pupils and the community of Treetown.

The previous paragraph contains the essence of the story. It tells the journalist the name of the school – Anytown Primary School, where it is based – Treetown, and the angle – the launch of £250,000 appeal to build a swimming pool. In essence the first paragraph needs to answer the who, what, where, when and how questions.

The second paragraph

This goes on to give the details already summarized in paragraph one: the facts and figures if necessary. You may only need one paragraph of explanation otherwise two will probably be sufficient.

Example – second paragraph

Anytown Primary School is launching the Swimalong Appeal to provide all children with the ability to swim on leaving the school. The school swimming pool is a vital facility as the village has many low-income families who are unable to afford travelling to nearby Cityland for swimming lessons. Anytown School's aim is that once built no child will leave the school unable to swim. After school hours, and during the summer holidays, the pool is to be made available to the whole village.

We could add in here another paragraph containing statistics of the number of children who drown because they couldn't swim, to strengthen our appeal.

The third paragraph
This is usually the quote.

Example of a third paragraph
Michael Diver, Head teacher, says, 'The swimming pool would be of great benefit to the local community as there are only limited recreation facilities available in Treetown. We have already received tremendous support for our Appeal from the pupils and parents of the school and are looking forward to holding a swimathon to celebrate when the pool is built. Ideally we would like this to be before next summer.'

The fourth paragraph
The fourth paragraph may contain practical facts.

Example of a fourth paragraph
Anyone wishing to donate to the Swimalong Appeal, or who would like to help raise funds, can contact Michael Diver on 023 921234.

After this you should write ENDS, and the date, 'For further information contact' and give details of contacts for the journalist or editor.

Keep your news release as simple as possible and factual. Do not use superlatives or unnecessary adjectives. Remember you are writing this as if you are the journalist and not someone from the school. If you need to say you're brilliant then put this in the quote.

Decide who is going to draft your releases, a teacher, someone on the governing body or on the fundraising committee, the head teacher, or deputy head? Ensure the head teacher reviews it before it is issued to the media.

Note to the editors

You may wish to include at the bottom of your news release, after the contact details, a short paragraph on notes to the editors. This should contain a few brief lines providing background on your school.

Laying out the news release

- simply type out **'News Release'** at the top of a piece of A4 paper or on your school headed notepaper if you prefer
- type neatly with 1.5 spacing and wide margins
- use only one side of paper. Your news release should be no longer than one and a half sides of A4, preferably one side of A4 paper.
- don't underline anything
- if you go onto a second page put 'more follows …' at the bottom of the first page
- don't split a sentence or a paragraph between one page and the next
- staple the pages together
- get someone to proof read it for mistakes before it goes out
- send by first class post, e-mail or fax and wherever possible address to the journalist by name.

Photographs

The newspapers, like many organisations, have experienced cutbacks and changing working practices over recent years. Some newspapers no longer retain a full-time, or even part-time, photographer but sub-contract this to freelancers so there is pressure on sending a photographer to your event. Yes, you can contact the newspaper and ask them if they would be prepared to send a photographer but the newspaper photographer has many calls upon his time and could be on an assignment that the editor views as more important than yours – a fire in a tower block is going to be more newsworthy than your school fund raising event even if the local MP is attending! You will increase your chances of getting into the newspaper or magazine if you take your own photograph and send it in with your news story. If you do, then ensure that your photograph is a close up shot. Most amateurs tend to favour the long shot – you know, someone sitting behind a desk and all you can see is acres of table and a tiny person at the end. This will never get into print.

If you have a group of people to photograph, get them to move very close together. They will feel awkward but it will make a better shot. Most magazines and newspapers crop shots and they can't do this if everyone is too spread out. Avoid the red eye and the scared haunted look.

Study the photographs in the newspapers and magazines you are targeting to see what style they like and try to emulate it. Most newspapers and magazines accept digital images e-mailed to them as a jpeg attachment.

Your launch news release should certainly go to the media with a photograph, which should show your fundraising appeal name and logo if you have one.

One of the reasons a company may wish to support your fundraising is because of the increased exposure to the media. A news release on how a company is helping you is usually welcomed by most businesses and often can be accompanied by a photograph. Try and avoid the traditional cheque presentation photograph though and think of something a little more creative if you can.

Some rules for good media relations

Do try and understand the media. Editors have a job to do and that job is to produce newspapers or magazines that their readers want to buy, or to broadcast programmes that people want to listen to and watch. Try and provide them with stories they will want and that are suitable for their medium.

Always try and be accessible. The media work to tight deadlines so if a journalist telephones you for a comment, or for further information, then try and ensure you are available to take that call or return it quickly. Failure to respond may mean missed coverage for your organisation. It is usually best to have a single point of contact within the organisation and someone who is usually on the premises, not always teaching or in meetings.

Don't hound a journalist to find out when your news story is likely to appear. They hate this. Besides if you do follow up the release you may not get the truth. It is not that the journalist will deliberately lie to you (although some may) it is just that they are under pressure and may genuinely not know if they will use the story. And even if they have decided to use it the editor may pull it because of more pressing items that have arisen during the day or the week. If your news story doesn't get taken up then don't worry and don't take it personally. First review what you have written to see if you can improve it for the next story. Did you have a good strong angle in the first paragraph? Is it easy to read? Is it short and simple? Is it interesting? Second, don't lose heart but keep looking for those good stories and keep sending them in; the journalist will soon realize you mean business and that you have some interesting news to tell.

In summary

- building a media profile can help you to fundraise
- you need to give the journalists your news in the format and language they like, i.e. in a News Release
- your first big story is the launch of your fundraising appeal, follow this up with a stream of other related news stories
- put media/news stories on the agenda of your fundraising committee meetings
- address your news release to a named journalist, first telephoning the publication to find out who
- research your local radio and television stories to find out who might be interested in your news story
- when constructing your news release think of a

triangle or pyramid; the angle, who you are and where you're based needs to be in the first paragraph, then flesh the story out with other details
- keep your news release as simple and factual as possible
- understand the media, they work to tight deadlines, try and be accessible or provide a contact for them who is not always teaching or in meetings
- if you fail to respond you will miss the opportunity for coverage
- don't hound a journalist to find out if your news story is going to appear, and if it doesn't, simply carry on with the next story.

14
Other ways of raising funds

Don't fall foul of the law

Many schools are not always fully aware of the law surrounding fundraising and it is easy to end up on the wrong side of the bench and incur financial penalties. A little bit of research beforehand could save a lot of money and hassle in the long run. So it is best to check out the rules and regulations before embarking on a number of initiatives. Here I attempt to summarize some of the key points for you but for further information check out the Charities Commission web site.

Street collections

Street collections are often more associated with the larger charities like Guide Dogs for the Blind and Cancer Research where people rattle a tin at you and you donate money in return for a sticker. While it may be unlikely that your school will embark on a street collection it isn't impossible. Your school may be situated in a small village or within a tight-knit community where standing outside the local Co-op with your tin might be deemed a good idea by some. If so, it might be more advisable if you are collecting for something specific like building a swimming pool or sports centre that could be used by the whole community, otherwise collectors could come in for some debate on the ethics of this mode of fundraising where a school is concerned!

Street collections, as defined by the Charities Commission, also include selling goods for charity in public places. This could include a private field where members of the public are invited. It can also include shopping malls, station forecourts, and supermarket car parks. However the latter are usually owned privately and therefore fall outside the controls on street collections. If in doubt check it out with the owner of the shopping centre or supermarket.

For street collections and for selling goods in public places (this may also apply to a school field you are using for a car boot sale) check out if you are required to get a permit or licence from your local authority.

For street collections you will need to give each collector written authority to collect on your behalf. You should not use collectors who are under 16 in England and Wales (14 in London with special consent), 14 in Scotland and 18 in Northern Ireland. Dress your collectors in an eye- catching way with sashes, tabards or costumes and hand out pins or stickers that don't damage clothes.

Carol singing

You might consider carol singing as a way of raising money for your school. As mentioned above most shopping centres are privately owned and therefore fall outside the legal requirements stated above. If the owner refuses you permission you can place your carol singers on the public pavement and the collectors on the private property. The act of singing on the pavement does not amount to a collection of money but it might be advisable to request a permit from your local authority and if they refuse, to notify the police.

House to house collections

These must have a licence granted either by the local authority or, if the collection is made in London, the local police or the Common Council of the City of London. Exemptions can be granted by the local police if it is for a very local collection to be completed within a short period of time. House to house collections also include visits made to pubs, offices and factories to appeal for money or to sell other things with the proceeds going to your charity.

In England, Wales and Northern Ireland collectors must be issued with a certificate of authority, a badge and a collecting box or receipt book with a number and a clear indication of the purpose of the collection. No collector can be under 16 (14 in Scotland) and money must be placed in the collecting box. An envelope collection requires the consent of the Home Secretary.

Collection boxes

There are no legislative controls over putting collecting boxes into local shops and pubs but there is a code of practice which has been drawn up by the Institute of Charity Fundraising Managers. You will need to obtain the written permission of the site holders to collect on their premises, issue certificates of authority and identity badges to collectors who are to site and service the boxes. Ensure that the boxes are of suitable material and are properly labelled, numbered and sealed and that they carry your registered charity number and charity name. Maintain records of where the boxes are sited and how much money is collected from each box and keep separate accounting records showing money raised and any direct expenses incurred in administering them.

Lotteries

There are many restrictions regarding lotteries and because it could be quite easy to fall foul of the law many schools may wish to avoid this area of fundraising with the possible exception of small lotteries.

A lottery is where you have a distribution of prizes and the distribution of those prizes has been done by chance. In addition the participants in the lottery must make a contribution to obtain the chance i.e. they buy a ticket or make a purchase of some kind.

There are two types of charity lotteries regulated by the Lotteries and Amusements Act 1976 as amended by the National Lottery Act 1993. These are:

Other ways of raising funds

- a small lottery
- a society's lottery.

Small lotteries

A small lottery must be genuinely incidental to what are called in the 1976 act 'exempt entertainment': these include fetes, bazaars, dinner dances and sales of work. There must be no cash prizes and the total value of prizes must not exceed £250. All the proceeds must be donated to the charitable cause. The sale and issue of tickets and the announcement of the winners must be made during the entertainment and on the premises where held.

Society lotteries

Society lotteries are probably not of interest to schools as they are promoting the sale of lottery tickets which will exceed £20,000 in value. If you do go ahead with a society lottery you will need to register with the Gaming Board and Trustees would be advised to contact the local authority and get further advice. Competitions such as bingo and the use of slot machines are also mainly regulated by the Gaming Board.

Free prize draws

Holding a free prize draw may be more attractive. To make sure that it falls outside the definition of a lottery you need to ensure that no donation i.e. actual contribution is necessary. A free prize draw therefore will only be lawful if instead of selling tickets you use them to solicit donations. You cannot enforce, impose or demand a sum of money or a donation. To make sure it is a lawful free prize draw you need to make clear on the tickets that no donation is necessary. You may like to suggest an amount alongside the 'no donation is necessary' but be careful of wording.

Prize competitions

This is another way to avoid the law on lotteries. However the competition itself cannot ask questions predicting the result of a future event, for example who will win the FA Cup. When framing questions the success should depend on the skill exercised by the participants. The marketing and advertising of a prize competition and rules of entry should comply with the Advertising Standards Code of Sales Practice.

To make sure you don't fall foul of the law, check it out. There are a number of very useful and easy to understand booklets available from the Charities Commission that cover the above areas, namely *Charities and Fund Raising* and *Charities and Trading*.

Trading is another area that you might like to explore i.e. selling items of clothing with your charity fundraising logo on them or other gifts to raise money for your cause.

You can obtain booklets on the above by visiting www.charity-commission.gov.uk or telephoning 0870 3330123. Another useful and very detailed book is *The Fundraisers Guide to the Law* which is published by the Directory of Social Change and costs £16.95, contact info@dsc.org.uk or telephone 020 7209 5151.

Other useful addresses for advice:

Gaming Board of Great Britain

Other ways of raising funds

Lotteries Section
Tel: 020 7306 6200

Institute of Charity Fund Raising Managers
Tel: 020 7627 3436

Advertising Standards Authority
Tel: 020 7580 5555
www.asa.org.uk

In summary

- check out the rules of fundraising before embarking on them, that way you won't fall foul of the law

15
Keep going

Instant results are not possible. It takes time and persistence.

Always look for opportunities

Keep your eyes and ears open, read avidly and approach anyone who might be even remotely interested in helping you. They can say no but they might say yes.

Network

Use your contacts and keep a high local profile amongst local education authority staff and council members. Know what is going on and who is who in your area. Continue to spot and capitalize on opportunities. Find out who is building or considering building in your area, for example commercial or housebuilding developers – can you approach them to see if they are interested in a bit of goodwill by helping your school? Contact the economic development manager on your council to find out which companies are interested in coming into your area. Approach them and ask for their help and suggest ways you can work in partnership.

Read the national press

Keep abreast of company developments and government initiatives. Are new grants about to be launched, or are new quangos, new trusts and foundations being established? If you get in early you might catch the worm!

Subscribe and read *Practical Funding for Schools* magazine which not only gives you ideas and tips but will keep you up to date with information on company giving, trusts and foundations and grants.

Maintain your media profile

This will help to keep you in the public eye and may even draw funding from that rich and famous person whose relative lives in your home town.

Build your database on donors and potential donors

Circulate copies of good press coverage to your supporters, keep them and donors informed of your progress. Compile a collage of press cuttings to send out with a newsletter to update people on your fundraising and your achievements. And always ask for money.

Say thank you promptly to funders

Send them a letter which thanks them but at the same time asks them to consider continuing to support you. Often people or companies that have donated once will donate again so keep in touch with them.

Explore other ways of generating income for your school like renting your school out on location for film crews, or offering facilities for conferences (if you have the right sort of premises and location).

Getting the first donation or grant is the hardest part of fundraising, but once one group of people give it is easier to attract other funders.

So:

- get yourself organized
- take advice if necessary
- read up on fundraising
- build your contacts and database
- do your research
- be methodical in your approach
- use your imagination to find and attract new sponsors and funders
- keep in touch with all possible funders and funders

> Be persistent, patient and professional.
> Good luck!

Useful addresses

Charity Commission
www.charity-commission.gov.uk
General Enquiries: 0870 333 0123

Inland Revenue (IR Charities)
Tel: 0151 472 6046 (Trading enquiries)
Tel: 0151 472 6036 (General enquiries)

For Scotland
Tel: 0131 777 4040
www. Inlandrevenue.gov.uk/charities/index/htm

Who's Who in Charities
CaritasData Limited
Paulton House
8 Shepherdess Walk
London
N1 7LB
Te: 0207 566 8210
www.caritasdata.com

Directory of Social Change
24 Stephenson Way

London
NW1 2DP
Tel: 020 7209 5151
E mail: books@dsc.org.uk
www.dsc.org.uk

Profunding
Suite 1.02
St Mary's Centre
Oystershell Lane
Newcastle upon Tyne
NE4 5QS
Tel: 0191 232 6942
Fax: 0191 232 6936
E mail: info@fundinginformation.org.
www.fundinginformation.org

Funderfinder
www.funderfinder.org.uk
Grantfinder
Enterprise House
Carlton Road
Worksop
Nottinghamshire S81 7QF
enquiries@grantfinder.co.uk
www.grantfinder.co.uk
Telephone: 01909 501200

First Monday
firstmonday-on@list.drfgroup.co.uk
DRF Group Limited
2440 The Quadrant
Aztec West
Almondsbury
Bristol BS32 4AQ
Tel: 01454 878 573
Fax: 01454 878 673

Practical Funding for Schools
Step Forward Publishing
The Coach House
Cross Road
Milverton, Leamington Spa
CV32 5PB
Tel: 01926 420046
Fax: 01926 420042
www.practicalfunding.com

Debretts People of Today
Debretts Peerage Limited
Kings Court
2-16 Goodge Street
London W1T 2QA
Tel: 020 7753 4213
www.debretts.co.uk
www.showcase-music.com
www.ukacts.com

UK Guide to Company Giving
(See Directory of Social Change)

Hollis Sponsorship and Donations Yearbook
Hollis Directories Limited
Harlequin House
7 High Street
Teddington Middlesex
Tel: 020 8977 7711
Fax: 020 8977 1133
www.hollis-pr.com

National Statistics Office
www.statistics.gov.uk

The Technology Colleges Trust
www.tctrust.org.uk

European Funding and the UK (Guide to Funding Process)
8 Storeys Gate
Westminster
London SW1P 3AT
Tel: 020 7973 1992
www.cec.org.uk

Charities Aid Foundation
www.cafonline.org

Institute of Fundraising
www.institute-of-fundraising.org.uk.

Neighbourhood Statistics Services
www.neighbourhood.statistics.gov.uk

The Big Lottery Fund
Head Office
1 Plough Place
London EC4A 1DE
Tel: 020 7211 1800
Fax: 020 7211 1750
general.enquiries@biglotteryfund.org.uk

South Africa

Southern Africa Institute of Fundraising National Office
SAIF
PO Box 1360
SANLAMHOF 7532
Tel: (021) 946 4110
www.geocities.com/Athens/Delphi/4594/?200515